LETTERS

Rudolph I Habsburg,
Holy Roman Emperor

Translated by: D.P. Curtin

Dalcassian Publishing Company

Copyright @ 2012 Dalcassian Publishing Company

All rights reserved. No part of this publication may be reproduced, distributed, or transmitted in any form or by any means, including photocopying, recording, or other electronic or mechanical methods, without the prior written permission of the publisher, except in the case of brief quotations embodied in critical reviews and certain other non-commercial uses permitted by copyright law. For permission request, write to Dalcassian Publishing Company at dalcassianpublishing at gmail.com

ISBN: 979-8-8689-2059-2 (Paperback)

Library of Congress Control Number:
Author: Curtin, D.P. (1985-)

Printed by Ingram Content Group, 1 Ingram Blvd, La Vergne, Tennessee

First printing edition 2012.

LETTERS

LETTERS

FIRST BOOK.

THE FIRST LETTER *Rudolph, elected king of the Romans, asks for the votes of the religious congregation to establish the auspices of his empire. (An. Dom. 1273, cod. Caes. 53, cod. Rud. I.)*

ARGUMENT.--Rudolphus, the chosen king of the Romans, anxious about attaining the imperial diadem, and terrified at the sight of the terrible Empire due to his long vacancy, begs the Cistercian nuns, reminded of his love and munificence, and inspired by the hope of royal patronage, to implore divine help for him with prayers.

Assumed divinely to direct the prayers of the Roman Empire, while in the lofty height of the mirror, to which the hand of the Lord has virtuously presided over us, let us turn our eyes to the face of the abyss below, while we see the hitherto uncultivated territory of the same empire all around, wild every day with the density of insurgent storms, apparently with a kind of fear as well as trembling [in horror] we are let down from the premises, rightfully trembling with uncertain fear. True, having sometimes rejected the primitive auspices of our sublimation, blinded to our consideration, paying attention to the fact that the hand of the Most High has advanced us from such low places of hut to such lofty, such [high and] lofty palaces in him whose admirable power gives by grace that things which are fragile by nature are stable. we place the hope of our confidence, presuming with confidence that the work, which the ineffable dispensation of his omnipotence is acknowledged, will be completed with a successful augury. Furthermore, since we consider the constant prayers of the righteous to be extremely necessary for us, we exhort your devotion more attentively, inasmuch as, observing with due gratitude, that in your actions the royal highness gladly aspires to you, commend us to divine clemency by the votes of your pious prayers.

LETTER II. *Fr. John, abbot general of the holy Cistercian order, replies to Rudolph's earlier letters recommending his order to himself. (An. Dom. 1273, cod. Rud. II.)*

ARGUMENT.--Brother John, abbot of Cistercian, replaces the royal letters, which were read in the general chapter, and heard by all with a joyful spirit, the hope of ancient love and patronage being confirmed. That the sacrifices of the Masses, and the state prayers for all the royal house, should be directed to the whole order of the Cistercians, whose privileges and remissions the kingdom commends to its patronage.

To the Most Serene Rudolph, chosen king of the Romans, brother John, who gives salvation to kings, may act successfully in him. Your Royal Highness's letter was received with due reverence and I read it before the assembled priests from different parts of the world. , not only were they heard more willingly and were more favorably understood, but their request also deserved to be heard effectively and cheerfully. Let your serenity know, therefore, that for the preservation of your health as well as [in] increase, for the most illustrious lady Anna, a sharer and consort of your magnificence, and also for your most illustrious offspring, to all and each of the brothers of our entire order, votes of other prayers have been imposed and enjoined , to be offered by them more willingly and speedily to divine clemency, by which they recognize you as a benevolent father, and their ardent zealot, whom perhaps from the abundance of your excellency I recommend more closely, for forgiveness of the same graces and favors, rising up to your thanks multiple actions, ready nevertheless to do them with a more prompt mind to complete according to the measure of his own ability, by the following effect, which having been received again of your well-pleasing will.

LETTER III. *Rudolph also asks the holy virgins for prayers for him and his wife. (An. Dom. 1273, cod. Rud. III.)*

ARGUMENT.--In the following two letters, written for the same reason and for the same purpose, to nuns of different orders, Rudolph asks for their fervent prayers, which he thinks will be effective, since they are directed to her Son Jesus Christ, most accepted by the nuns of the most holy Virgin.

Raised to the mirror of royal dignity by the divine ordinance, while we pay careful attention to the importunable burdens resting on our shoulders, while in the balance of continuous meditation we weigh our own weakness and insufficiency of strength, and when we undertake the work we look at the gravity, such [that already] we are compelled to marvel with fear and trembling, and the preeminence of the steps, and fearing the face of the abyss seen below, lest perhaps the terrible height of the place should generally frighten us, yet we are relieved by the confidence of divine clemency, hoping that we may pass through the distresses of this spacious and stormy sea unscathed, if you obtain for us the help of salvation and grace, which are the heavenly bridegroom in your conscience You have prepared a flowery bed of delights. For what will be denied you by divine piety, which [although] you always deserve to have the propitiation of the virtues and the fragrance of the works of the blessed [Blessed?]. What will your heralds not be able to obtain from the shining queen mother of God, by whose merits the Church shines, the world flourishes by examples, and the Christian religion advances? What will not that most illustrious line of citizens obtains from your votive affections, which is returned to you in propitiation for the praises of God and for the merits of an innocent life? Behold, then, we who, with Martha, are disturbed by many perplexities and inconveniences, waiting for the appropriate comfort of help from those who are at peace with Mary, your university, which we presume to have the grace of the eternal king and the favor of the heavenly court with clear evidence, we have led the petitioners to demand, inasmuch as we and the famous Anna, queen of the Romans, our dearest consort having obtained the grace of divine omnipotence by your pious interventions, so that his wonderful power may make strong by grace what are fragile by nature; may he support our weakness with strength, and strengthen him with strength; and grant us to pursue from on high what he has committed and delivered, in so far as the growth of his glory is strengthened, and the Christian people may sit together with us in the beauty of peace and opulent rest, illuminated at last by the rays of perpetual glory.

LETTER IV. *The same with the above argument and written in almost the same words. (An. Dom. 1273, cod. Rud. IV.)*

In the honor of the exalted dignity with which the exalter of the lowly has preferred us, it is as if an immovable burden is tied to our shoulders, whose venerable and stupendous greatness we consider, we do not undeservedly fear. But just as we are drowned by the consideration of our frailty, so we are in a way relieved by the confidence of divine clemency, hoping that we may successfully cross the traps of this stormy sea, if you obtain for us the help of salvation, who have prepared a flowery bed for the heavenly bridegroom in the delights of your conscience. For what will be denied to you by the mercy of God to those who deserve it to have propitiation in the whiteness of the virtues? What won't your conversation achieve with the shining queen, mother of God's angels, the glorious lady, by whose merits the Church shines, and the Christian religion thrives and prospers by their examples? What will that line of the blessed not obtain by your votive affections, which is rendered propitiatory to you, and for the praises of the divine announcements, and the merits of an innocent life? Behold, that you have the grace of the eternal king and the favor of the heavenly court, it is presumed by clear arguments, and confirmed by clear signs. Therefore we beseech you with dignity through the mercy of God, inasmuch as by pious meditation we consider as much as possible from it the threat of astonishment, that we who bear the essence of dust and ashes, have become the vicars of the ruler for ages by the temporal sword, by the protection of your pious prayers obtain for us the votes of divine grace, by humble supplication asking that his wonderful power, by his grace to be the strongest that is weak by nature, support our weakness with strength, and fill it with strength, and thus grant us to carry on what he delivered to our impotence, and committed to humility, inasmuch as he passes into the increase of his glory, and the Christian people may peace and tranquility proceed through us, and finally may the ray of eternal glory shine upon them and upon us.

LETTER V. *Rudolph, elected king of the Romans, writes to reform all the states of the empire for peace, and to show them the obedience due to him. (An. Dom. 1273, cod. Rud. V.)*

ARGUMENT.--Supplied for divine help by religious men and holy virgins, thinking seriously about restoring the Roman Empire to the excised things, the encyclical in this letter invites all the leaders of the same empire, both ecclesiastical and lay, to pay homage and the sacrament of fidelity.

By the vocation of him called to the helms of the Roman kingdom, who removes the pride of the lofty peaks, and places the devoted humility of the lowly in the lofty, we prepare our minds and turn with watchful meditation, how in the high, very high and lofty king of kings, seated on the throne of the majesty of kings, we consult for the reformation of the peace of the long-disintegrated republic, and those who have been oppressed until now , and let us beware of the costly dangers of the tyranny of tyrants. Hence it is that since we are placed in the highest glasses of dignity, that all the members of the holy Roman Empire, and those who bear faith in us through devoted services, should contemplate our serenity with clear obscurity and sincere affections, all of you, and each one of you, with all the kindness that befits serenity. we embrace the royal one, believing with a gracious heart, and presuming without any scruple of ambiguity, that our affection, which you will be able to experience from the grace of our serenity which is expended upon you, should receive every kind of recompense through you, through the devout obedience of your fidelity.

LETTER VI. *A certain city congratulates Rudolph on his election, and thanks him for the remission of offences, commending himself to him. (An. Dom. 1273, cod. Rud. VI.)*

ARGUMENT.--The city of Basle, recently besieged by the arms of Rudolph, liberated soon after receiving the news of the election, and writing to them with letters full of benevolence and hope of benefits, testifies to great joy, thanksgiving, oblivion of the past, and due submission and obedience. Finally, he begs him to confirm his laws and good customs.

Rejoicing and congratulating with all our hearts, and praising the unconquered Germany, that after various calamities and hardships, the king of heaven, looking down from the abode of the heavens on high, deigned to visit the election of the Roman prince in divine truth rather than in human mercy. Indeed, the ingenuity of the race and manners of the prince, the excellent courage of the mind, and the indefatigable magnanimity have been impressed upon the ears of those who dwell in remote parts of the world by the fame. Moreover, since out of the abundant grace of the royal majesty, you were deigned to direct your writings to us undeservedly, between the sweet words of the king and the restraint of clemency manifestly, that whatever grudge against our city existed towards you, completely relegated to the scruple of the whole future question, you remitted with royal kindness. Wherefore, to the serenity of your excellency, we rise humbly bowing with all that we are capable of in the kind of graces, all deeply offended, which to us universally and individually, before the Lord summoned you to the summit of the imperial pinnacle, for the quality of the times you have brought, remitting completely and entirely, that is, to the perpetual rust of oblivion superimposed, recalling to memory that poem: He who could hurt, will sometimes be able to benefit. Wherefore we beseech your majesty's majesty with all our strength and affections, inasmuch as by your liberal kindness in preserving the rights of our commonwealth, and the good custom which is a suitable interpreter of the laws, as the letters lately sent to us from your serenity promise, you will continue us, as we hope, with favor special grace, since we are also ready, and intend to be inviolable, to faithfully execute your majesty's orders and commands, as was just and consistent with equity, for the quality of our forces.

LETTER VII. *Another city also congratulated Rudolph on his election as king of the Romans, commending itself to him in submission. (An. Dom. 1274, cod. Rud. VII.)*

ARGUMENT.--When Rudolphus, having received the crown of the Germanic kingdom at Aachen, through the provinces under the rule of Rom. he had sent the subjects news, that they would receive homage from the states of the whole of Germany, one of them, delaying it, adorns an embassy to Rudolph, which functions in that function more magnificently. The praises of the crowned king are lavished upon him; He gives thanks to Almighty God that he has freed himself from the tyranny of the invaders, and he imploringly requests that his subjection to the ecclesiastical prince, confirmed by the agreements agreed upon, be moderated.

Blessing, glory, wisdom, and thanksgiving, honor, virtue, and strength to him who sits on the throne, who lives forever and ever. Who, at the dawn of the world, in our Roman days, the monarchy of the empire, already tottering as if on feet of clay, adorned with a golden head, crowned with honor and glory as a king. Whom the king of kings, rich over all, who anointed him above all his consorts, with the prudence of Solomon's silver breast, and with riches, with the victorious steel of a military sword, and with the brazen herald of all virtues, may he make stable in all the earth, and to the ends of the earth, in his predestined dominion, and through glorious centuries To this imperial majesty of yours, our singular and universal master of the whole world, approaching with confidence to the throne of grace, we confidently offer the city, all our substance, and our persons, certain that we shall find grace in the opportune assistance, which for a long time has been possessed by foreign masters, to whom a vague right that is, we were in miserable slavery. Therefore, let the clemency of the king's throne be established, and while we are converted from strangers to our own from many to one master, since our temporal salvation is only in your hand, O Lord, let the eyes of your mercy look upon us, that we may serve our king most joyfully. Of course, the fact that we did not make this profession of due service and fidelity as required by your majesty's messages was nothing else than the occasion of delay, except that we were affected to present ourselves personally to the sight of your majesty by the bearers of the present, whom we chose from all of us on account of their honesty, the service of our legation in your to be prosecuted by the imperial court. For this we need as much as possible, so that we may take care on our behalf of the faith recited, while you claim imperial jurisdiction over us, that commission and agreement, by which the king of the Romans N. then the governor of the empire, subjected us to the venerable lord N. The aforesaid prince shall have no action against us, unless, indeed, for your supreme excellency he is our helper in opportune necessities.

LETTER VIII. *Someone writes to Rudolph, and the great work of the pontiff and his wonderful sublimation of the state of the church and the empire, which had hitherto collapsed, will be reformed (An. Dom. 1274, cod. Rud. VIII.)*

ARGUMENT.--In an allegorical description of the long interregnum after Frederick II., while the tyrants, feloniously, the irreligious, perverted all divine and human rights, he says, by the mercy of God, that Gregory X, established in the see of Peter, was conspicuous for his virtue and sanctity, as if the sun and

Rudolph were like the moon in a fluctuating government tribute: the common hope of all, that both of the luminaries will be restored to their former serenity.

The wisdom of the divine plan, which, of course, is the secret circle of the heavens alone, uncreated, the first parent feeling that he is being driven to posterity by discrimination, and by the exorbitation of his own plasma, which in a certain way embraces the natural norm of transgression, irritated, usually suffers the weakness of the human race, now pestilence, now disaster, now involved the waves of the war storm. The moon, indeed, for a long time seemed to have been lifted from the sky, condensed into the shadowy mist of darkness, and it became a heavy night, and full of dangers, in which the beasts of the forest passed in groups, the cubs of lions roaring, that they might abduct the innocent. But in the midst of Egypt, in a mixed spirit of vertigo, the truth had come into oblivion, the keys of Peter had somehow fallen into contempt, the liberties of the Church had been trampled upon by a furious tyranny. But the Most High Mediator of God and men, who was not wont to restrain mercy in anger, after the manifold distresses of terrible persecution, by which the world was torn and withered, by which the bonds of Christianity were loosened, shaken by the expenses of the split, thus having compassion on the afflicted, pitying the misery of the afflicted, has already seen the tears of the faithful with the gracious right hand to wipe away the consolation, and to restrain the mournful lamentations of the sobbing. For he placed in the apostolic seat a man according to his own heart, like a most splendid solar star, outshining the preeminence of virtue, the works of holiness, and the rays of justice. In your sublimation too, any faithful and equal interpreter can judge of the wonderfulness that, restored by the divine nod of the light of the lunar globe, the cloudy mists of the state of the empire that had hitherto wavered are cleared away, the delightful serenity of the faithful of both luminaries shines forth more clearly and radiatingly in the universal expectation, that Jerusalem may be restored as it was in the days of the ancients, and their deserts are set as delights, and solitudes impassable as gardens.

LETTERS

LETTER IX. *A certain prince writes to the supreme pontiff about the election of Rudolph, recommending him to him. (An. Dom. 1274, cod. Rud. IX.)*

ARGUMENT.--Prince N. exaggerating the calamities of the same interregnum, and understanding that Rudolph was divinely chosen as king of the Romans to punish the wicked, but to reward the good; Gregory X earnestly prays that he may be present to the same king, for the establishment of peace, the extermination of heretical corruption, and the spread of the orthodox faith in Syria.

I am not unmindful of the dignity of human knowledge of its primitive origin, because all were born free from the beginning, and did not recognize the preeminence of the president, it seemed to shake off the yoke of slavery, and to refute the preeminence of dominion. Indeed, the unpunished license of criminals, giving an incentive to the malevolent to transgress, had sown so many seeds of malice in the fields of the mother Church, that the poisonousness of nettles and other noxious herbs seemed to suffocate Dominic's wheat. Therefore, looking forward from heaven to reward the merits of the just and repress the wickedness of the perverse, he presided over the law on earth, out of the depth of his counsel, lord Rudolphus, the serenest king of the Romans, to be respected by all mortals, as regards temporal things, from whom, as the reason of the law commands, a fief together with my sons. nor was I received by the princes of the Eastern parts with the solemnity which was due, and manifest. I beseech your most pious fatherhood, inasmuch as with the fullness of favor to my said lord, and with the affection of kindness usual, both fatherly and piously assist the good state of the Christian people, that the lost peace may flourish again, heretical perversity may rejoice, and the planting of the orthodox faith against the rivals of Christ's cross may expand to the glory of Christ.

LETTER X.
A certain city rejoices at Rudolph's promotion, devoting itself entirely to him. (An. Dom. 1274, cod. Rud. X.)

ARGUMENT.--One of the so many provincial states of the empire, trusting that it had emerged from the tyranny of the invader, renders due obedience to Rudolphus; He commends the imperial dignity according to the opinion of that age, and the office of emperor as a manly one

It is not surprising if we give glory and honor to the Lord incessantly for your promotion, since he brought us the pearl from his talent, and this does not without reason yield us to the fullness of joys, when the Lord mercifully providing for us by nodding to our desires, shaking off the rust, brought us silver the purest vessel, the trust of our captivity and the redeemer of our extermination. For before the mountains were made, or the earth and the world were formed, it was predestined from the first age, that you should reside on the throne of imperial majesty, before whose tribunal the natural and civil laws tremble, the willingly heard conscience is revealed, incompetence is discovered, justice is strengthened, and iniquity is put to flight. Hence all who boast of the Christian name must, and can, resort to the clemency of your imperial majesty, with fuller confidence. For the Lord has given you the power of the temporal sword, that it may be your own serenity to bind the world of the earth to the bridle of law and justice, and also of equity. For the Lord has made you an emperor in the lands, whom we recognize as the Lord, and to whom our city is subject, so that you may be a shield against the enemies of the faith, a defender of justice, a lover of equity, an exterminator of malice, a pacifier of scandal, and a refuge for the powerless. For the power of Caesar does not abandon those who hope in justice, it relieves the oppressed, it supports the relieved, it protects widows, it protects orphans, it defends the weak, it comforts the weak, it raises up the prostrate, and it strengthens the upright in strength.

LETTER XI. *He has welcoming congratulations made to him. (An. Dom. 1274, cod. Rud. XI.)*

ARGUMENT.--N. The bishop received a congratulatory letter by the legate and followed it with much praise. Their opinion, and the ambassadors, acting in their capacity, provide an interpretation that he will never put down from memory; and he promises to always support himself and the Church committed to him.

Your placid words of congratulation to us upon the successful auspices of our sublimation, with a certain voluntary display of gratitude and gratuitous devotion, presented to us by the lovely speech of our lately culminating sweetness, have refreshed our hearts with an immense fragrance of delight, from the sweetness of their mellifluous nature. Indeed, he infused the theme with the praise of the words, so beautiful the hare in the bush, and to the excellent beauty of the sentences was added the savory flavor of the root, so that if (which is far from) even further consequence no fruit ever bursts forth from the flowers, yet the stream of hope does not cease to remain from the premisses. Of course, we kindly received your message from your ambassador, who proposed the words of his ambassador discreetly and providentially, and we made it a more tenacious memory to commend both what the message itself proposed and what the letter contained, the integrity of your faith and the purity of mind, which we consider you to have incessantly to advance the royal titles, proceeding more richly actions of thanks; and, nevertheless, in your actions and those of your Church, and in your opportunities, you will experience us as ultraneous and devoted.

LETTER XII. *Rudolph thanked Pope Gregory X most for having kindly listened to his appeal to the chancellor, promising that he would always be the most obedient son of the Roman Church. (An. Dom. 1274, cod. Rud. XII.)*

ARGUMENT.--Rudolphus Gregory X., for having kindly heard Otto his legate in the consistory of Lyons, gives abundant thanks; He promises filial obedience in all things; He promises to come to the holy land, where the ashes of his father rest, with a strong protection. He was very desirous of conversing with him about making peace between the Christians. His controversy with the Count of Savoy, an interpreter being sent on both sides, was to be delegated to the discretion of the Pontiff. All the princes, barons, and others throughout Alemagne behave themselves; and it means that he will completely submit to the pontifical commands.

Most loving father of fathers, from all the children of men above all who live under our mortality in a habit of reverence, in your rising praise heralds, not that we are bound, but the actions that we can report abundant thanks for that which is the purpose of our sincere devotion, or readiness by a man certainly commendable. (Otto put forward) in the presence of your sanctity and your brothers, you listened more clemently to what was explained and offered, and you considered the proposals more kindly with the usual grace of piety. Because of this, we, in a solid [unsolid] persistently purposeful heart, with a pure [pure heart], not a fake conscience, for the honor of God and the exaltation of the Roman Church always want to be found in all efforts to be found, to encourage all churches and ecclesiastical persons with the continuation of favor, in presenting justice to them easy-going, and in conferring grace, as befits the honor of government, liberal, with every effort to root out the root of discord for the universal peace of the world, and to filially obey the pleas and commands of the apostolic see in avoiding matters of dissension. Driven by a fervent spirit in the desire of the mind, that of your holy land, by the counsel of your goodness to us, or by supporting the help which the only begotten Son of

God preferred to all the parts of the world, and by consecrating it, reddened it with the sprinkling of his most holy blood, both powerfully and openly [patiently] help, that [whereby the people of God, afflicted for many times by the enemies of the cross of Christ, and constrained to the glory of Christ, may be able to fearlessly visit the tomb of the Lord. Whereupon the ardor of longing is kindled in us all the more intensely, as the bones of our natural parent, for the glory of the crucified, resting there abroad alone outside of his birth, are turned more anxiously every day in our hearts. , who surrendered himself to exile and misery to the delights of paradise? But among the rest, the most desirous desire is to have an untiring desire to have a conversation with you, and to discuss how the peace, which has long been scattered, may be restored among the Christians. Above all the treaties, through the sweetness of your sweet piety, with our chancellor, offering our soul, body, honors, possessions, and everything to your well-pleasing sanctity. And in order that the word may be in harmony with the gratitude of the work, with the devout kisses of your beatitude's feet, when it pleases you, we wish to meet, and to enjoy the sight of your most holy person face to face. In regard to this controversy, which is between us on the one side, and the most illustrious Count of Savoy, who is faithful to you, on the other, has turned, amicably, or through justice through mediation, without noise, we both agreed that we, one, and the Count himself, on the other, will send suitable men to your court. , who will have full power to agree with us in turn. But to those who are not able to agree on a single opinion, we both promise to stand by the word of your will in good faith, having a certain confidence in the Lord, that from now on, after God, we will have no refuge or respect for any other than you and the sacred Roman Church, because all our affairs as the most beloved children, you will always have a paternal recommendation. And that the auspiciousness of our successful successes may not now be hidden from you, let it be known to you present, that the princes, barons, cities, camps, and other possessions of the sacred empire throughout Alemannia submit unanimously to our dominion. We therefore beseech your most holy piety, in so far as those who believe in the words of N. deign to reveal to us your well-pleasing will by the ministry of the living voice.

LETTER XIII. *Rudolph thanks a certain cardinal for favoring his part in the Roman court alone. (An. Dom. 1274, cod. Rud. XIII.)*

ARGUMENT.--NSRE thanks the cardinal, whom he knew, referring to his legates, that in the consistory of Lyons it was firmly and constantly of the opinion that, after Alphonsus had settled, his election should be considered approved; and he prays that, having laid the foundation, he may take care to complete the lofty summit, that is to say, the imperial majesty may be transferred to him from the supreme pontiff.

It has come to us a dance of immense joy, that where no cause of our merits had preceded, no knowledge of your familiarity had preceded, only, as we firmly believe, by the instinct of divine kindness, you so raised your arms towards ours, that, as we have received from a faithful narrative, you threw with a faithful hand the first stone, and the first step you have laid, on which the ladder of our promotion rests, and for the arduous ascent more solid foundations have already appeared to rise. Therefore, excellent father, having passed over the praises of which your perfection has deserved to be commended many times over, we bow down to you from the bottom of our hearts to the gratitude we can, we implore your paternity, inasmuch as you are determined to conclude the laudable principles begun around us with a more laudable means and the most excellent end from the innate excellence of goodness . For you can safely obtain the fullness of confidence from us, because we know that, according to the advice of your prudence, we are specially empowered to accept everything that the sacred Roman Church, our most pious mother, has received, and we constantly burn in your favors with filial reverence.

LETTER XIV. *He offers the abbot primary prayers for the ecclesiastical benefit by conferring something. (An. Dom. 1274, cod. Rud. XIV.)*

LETTERS

ARGUMENT.--In the four following epistles, observing the ancient custom, he offers primary prayers to the abbot, chapter, and bishop for the benefice or for a vacant canonry, or for a vacant one as soon as possible. The reluctant abbot is encouraged by royal authority. In the same way, without consulting the bishop in the holy see, he denies that this can be done with repeated prayers, and he attacks the proposals with the hope of love and grace.

While at the beginning of our sublimation every church established in the Roman Empire on the provision of one person is obliged to admit the first fruits of our kingdoms from the ancient and approved custom of the sacred empire, we offer you our primary prayers, exhorting your devotion more attentively, and commanding you nevertheless with royal authority, in so far as the bearer of the present, to the increase of whose honors and advantages, not only, the merits of his probity, but also the acceptance of his paternal, and not even his grandfather's energetic obedience, have effectually provoked us. Regarding the sufficient knowledge recommended to us, regarding the ecclesiastical beneficence concerning your contribution, if there is a vacancy for the present, or as soon as the opportunity presents itself, you will take care to provide liberally, out of special respect for us and for the sacred government, so that from then on we are obliged to enlarge you and your church with dignified honors.

LETTER XV. *Secondarily, but with threats, he interrupts the abbot from conferring the same ecclesiastical benefice for which he had previously interceded. (An. Dom. 1274, cod. Rud. XV.)*

It may be otherwise that we direct our primary prayers for N., that according to the ancient and approved custom of ecclesiastical beneficence regarding your contribution you may study liberally to provide, you by our commands and prayers of this kind, Not paying attention to the fact that the same royal prayers contain in themselves the appearance of commands, you refused to admit them, as he made known to us. Wherefore we have once more affectionately exhorted your devotion, and admonished you, commanding you by royal authority, inasmuch as you are doing it out of necessity, for the said benefit, if there is anything available for the present, or as soon as the opportunity presents itself, you will take care to provide liberally. We shall preserve our right in this respect in such a way that we shall be the more favorably led to review your rights and those of your monastery in turn, and that it is not necessary for us to seek a spur against you on this.

LETER XVI. *Same with the previous two arguments. (An. Dom. 1274, cod. Rud. XVI.)*

The resplendent serenity of the royal majesty thus protects and protects the rights and customs of others, which is given and preserved to each one as his own. How much more is royal majesty itself obliged to defend its own rights, which it strives to preserve for others? Therefore, since the ancient and approved right of our predecessors, the divine emperors and kings, the custom that each person in each cathedral and other collegiate churches should be admitted to the primary royal prayers as canons and brothers, to be provided, when opportunity presents itself, will be obtained. We, following in the footsteps of our predecessors, direct our prayers to you through N. primary, asking with all urgency and affection, commanding nevertheless by royal authority, in so far as the fitness of the person is considered, that you will not refuse to receive him into your canonized college with the honor of our love, if any is now provided he is free, or as soon as he has the opportunity to do so, to contribute to himself, ceasing every opportunity. Doing in such a way that, while you do not diminish the royal rights, it may please the royal clemency not to diminish the freedom of your church, but to increase it, and it is not necessary to direct our writings to you on the promotion of the aforesaid No. repeated.

LETTER XVII. *Recommends to the bishop a certain primary prayer for a canon. (An. Dom. 1274, cod. Rud. XVII.)*

If you look carefully at the honor and beauty of the Roman Empire, which deserved to be placed in the eyes of all the princes, as if in a mirror, as from which the princes themselves contract the insignia of the principality, being enlarged by the bounties of his bounties , and endowed with the prerogative of honors; if, finally, you weigh in the balance of your consideration, how much place the discreet man N. has held in our court for you and your church up to now, and will be able to hold in the future, you will certainly not hesitate, nor waver as a doubt, unless you hold to his promotion from several reasons. Indeed, no corner of the empire is hidden, except from the ancient and approved custom of the empire, the provision of one person is owed to us and to our predecessors, the divine emperors and kings of the Romans, by any of the ecclesiastical prelates. For this reason we do not believe that it is necessary that apostolic authority is required for the reception and provision of N. in your church, because the N. church from the other churches of our kingdom, which have provided and provide incessantly with appropriate readiness for those for whom we have offered our primary prayers, it does not differ in the disparity of conditions, nor is it supported by the privilege of any exemption. And hence it is that we have led your fraternity to be exhorted with full affection, inasmuch as you will give applause in harmony with our right and the government, to receive the aforesaid N. by royal letters as a canon and as a brother, to be provided according to the order of his reception. For this will not prejudge the church, nor serve those who have received it, but will preserve with us, both for you and for him, the accumulation of favor and grace, and will claim the abundance of more fruitful benevolence. But what your will and intention finally came to be upon this, do not fail to make clear to us through the medium of the present.

LETTER XVIII. *Remits services not provided by the vacant government. (An. Dom. 1274, cod. Rud. XVIII.)*

ARGUMENT.--He pardons the services or tributes due to the government in respect of fiefs, and other goods of the government, which have been spent on account of the wars which have broken out, during the whole period of the interregnum, to the faithful princes or barons of P. and H.

Our serenity judges worthy, and decrees that, just as there is distinction between persons and places, so the merits of each should be treated differently, and the quality of retribution should be different, and grace and favor should be increased to each one as much as his submissive fidelity is known to predominate over the rest. Since therefore we know that you, P. and H., are so devoted and so faithful to the Holy Roman Empire, that there is no small certainty about those like you, we are equally desirous of bestowing on you the gift and bounty of special grace, all the services which, during the time of the vacant empire until our creation, to whomsoever you ought to have spent on the emperor or the king, whatever you received from the goods of the empire in the middle of the time on the occasion of the wars which oppressed you, we will mercifully and liberally indulge you all this out of royal kindness, not inflicting on you any punishment for your fault, or the threat of punishment in any degree, but you rather in all favor and the grace of abundant consolation and protection by comforting grace.

LETTER XIX. *He is grateful for the congratulations given to him. (An. Dom. 1274, cod. Rua. XIX.)*

ARGUMENT.--The prince, the baron, or any nobleman of Germany, who promises to attend the solemnity of the coronation, places himself in charge, in return, to take care of things conducive to the increase of that honor.

Our serenity has lately heard, whence a new joy has been accumulated for us, whence the matter of renewed delight has increased, because you, indeed, whom native virtue and powers together with the brightness of a noble blood, brought together the bliss of a more fortunate auspiciousness, as if to some embracing individuals, congratulating with an applauding affection the auspices and summits of our sublimation , for which you are willing to spend and present benevolent things, which will increase the titles of our honor, and the progress will be more open. Wherefore, having been provoked in a reciprocal turn to all things, in truth, which in like manner may add to your growth, to all things which may soften your spirits, we expose ourselves to you as insolent, and offer ourselves in conformity.

LETTER XX. *The Pisans invite Rudolph to quell the movements of Thuscia. (An. Dom. 1274, cod. Rud. XX.)*

ARGUMENT.--An address to the legate of the city of Pisa, in which he begs the king of the Romans in the name of the whole city over and over again to come to Italy as soon as possible to calm the internal discords of the citizens. This would be acceptable to not a few nobles driven from their country, and especially to the Roman Pontiff.

Laws assert, custom approves, antiquity protests, that the region of the Tuscians should serve under tribute to the Roman prince, to say nothing of the rest. Relying therefore on this consideration, one for many, alone for many, I speak to you, who am believed to be in the presence of the prince an intercessor for all. Behold, the province of Thusia, which, owing to its proximity to the pious seat of the Roman empire, ought to have answered more familiarly to its chief as its principal member, lies in a multitude of schisms, torn by wars, and more than by civilians. Twins collide in the womb, and at last malice prevails in Jerusalem, while the enemy is the friend, the stranger is the domestic, the Guelph pursues the Ghibelline, the children become exiles, and are exiled to a place of exile worthy of exile. The city of Pisa mourns, wounded by the hostile sword of the high pontiff and the royal crown. To whose protection the royal highness is believed to be so bound, and to yearn more ardently for the repulsion of his grievances, inasmuch as he clung to his highness from his progenitors by the purity of a firmer faith and is itself sublimated by the privilege of greater grace. Therefore, the royal highness is excited to speed the arrival, to be imitated by the favors of not a few Gentiles, and to be embraced by the arms of the apostolic deity, lest our enemies mock us any further because of the delay of our arrival.

LETTER XXI. *Rudolph Caesar responds to Pisani. (An. Dom. 1275, cod. Rud. XXI.)*

ARGUMENT.—Rudolph retorts that he sent his legate to the pontiff, together with the legate of the republic of Pisa, that he might comply with their wishes by the same not dissenting.

We kindly received your industrious man N., your ambassador, lately appointed by you to the presence of our majesty, and we gladly heard your words put into his mouth and committed, carefully and lawfully presenting them with eloquent speech. Of course, since it is easily applied to our intelligence whatever may be poured out for the increase and advantage of your generality and specialty, to your request, extended by him to our summit, willingly and liberally bending our benevolent ears, we direct our message together with your message to the court of the lord pope, that he may be pleased with it. and by agreement your final wishes may be fully satisfied upon what your petition contained. For we are prepared, and we shall try to be vindictive to you, in whatever way, according to the apostolic favor, the grace of honor and convenience may yield to you an increase.

LETTER XXII. *Rudolph sends an ambassador to the Pope. (An. Dom. 1275, cod. Rud. XXII.)*

ARGUMENT.--After the death of Otto, in charge of Spire and Rudolph the chancellor, and his orator to the pontiff, he sends another, who deals chiefly with Gregory about the imperial coronation, and other matters both of the empire and of his own.

Most, most blessed father, the mysteries of the interpreter of the Scriptures, in which filial devotion is represented by paternal aspects, have hitherto flowed from the pen of our breast, the affection of the inner mind, which we invariably bear towards the sacrosanct Roman Church, our mother, more imperfectly indicating and insufficiently expressing our wish. Because, therefore, the desires of the absent are more fully and plainly explained by the living voice of the oracle, than by the silent annotation of letters; Behold, we entrust the honorable man N., distinguished by much virtue, endowed with morals and knowledge, accepted by us by the merits of his honesty, to you also and devoted to the Roman Church at the feet of your beatitude, imploring your sanctity, inasmuch as he, whom we already believe in the truth of his predecessor by his laudable action to have a distinguished follower, and also a successor, with the dignity of propitiation, with which it is due, recommitted, to the same upon our principal and the business of the empire, and also upon other equally just petitions which he has presented to your holiness, I will more kindly invest the effect of a gracious hearing and a favorable hearing.

LETTER XXIII. *Rudolph asks the supreme Roman pontiff to lend him three thousand marks. mutual (An. Dom. 1275, cod. Rud. XXIII.)*

ARGUMENT.--Rudolph receiving from Gregory twelve thousand marches gratis for the equipment of the expedition to Syria; he asks for another three thousand to be drawn up for him, with a due guarantee. Moreover, he writes that he has chosen a strong leader, whom he will soon send with the troops into Etruria, as the pontiff had requested.

If we speak with the salutary reverence of your paternal benevolence, with no spirit of displeasure raised in your pious hearts, of that subsidizing expenses of fourteen thousand marks, in which you have so liberally provided for us, and for which filial devotion inclines fervently to your abundant gratitude, it seems to us from probable conjectures , that considering the magnitude of the business being undertaken, and considering the brevity of the time, the very support of such a large and famous apparatus is considered somewhat insufficient. We ask, therefore, with a face of shame and blushing, in so far as no difficulty may be thrown upon the aforesaid business, which after God the most powerful apostolic right directs, to add to the aforesaid twelve thousand three more indignity in the name of a loan, having previously, however, received a suitable guarantee. For we have already taken care to provide you with a magnanimous captain, or governor, who, having been proved by circumspection, who, gathering together a suitable army, to preside over and benefit in Thusia, having been overcome by the horrors of the ancient calamity, will direct his steps from the trail to that province, etc.

LETTER XXIV. *He sends the Count of Furstemberg, a pilot, into Italy. (An. Dom. 1275, cod. Rud. XXIV.)*

ARGUMENT.--Rudolph thinking that the Exarchate and Pentapolis, which in his time belonged to the Romandiola and the Maritimes, were under the right of the government, entrusts those provinces to the duke of Furstemberg, whom he then commends to the states.

Rudolph, etc. To the illustrious and prudent men, the marquises, counts, nobles, captains of states, powers, elders, and all the peoples appointed throughout Romania and the Maritimes, their health and good will. In a special way, among so many waves of falling business, with which the material of thought is constantly infused into our breast, we are filled with meditation, and we meditate with watchful anxiety, such as that noble region of Romaniola and the Maritimes, as a glorious orchard of empire, in which the royal majesty, from the charm of its peaceful worship, He was not satisfied with the least pleasure, let him flourish again and again, and after the terrible and long fatigue of the hostile straits, and the extraordinary tempests of war, in the port of votive tranquility and the beauty of peace, he rests. In this country indeed the government recognizes its students. For this is the sweet garden of the empire, in which he gathers the vernal and blooming flowers of a pleasing subject and plucks the pleasing apples of the devout sweetness. Of course, therefore, a curious attention is turned to the worship and protection of the royal highness himself, and the study of a more inclined vigilance is used, so that she too may breathe the fragrance of sincere purity through devotion and may return the expected fruit of constancy through complete fidelity. It is true that at that time the region is governed usefully, while it is directed by the direct leadership of the rector, and governed by the energy of the police president, we are desirous that the province itself rejoices in the supervision of the leader, our illustrious H. Count of Furstemberg, our kinsman, whose merits on the part of supervision and faith render him lovable to us, and proven vigor makes it more clear, we appoint you and all the pre-specified provinces as governor of the same province, committing ourselves fully to the execution of the kingdom in place of our name, so that his studious leadership may be preserved from harm and may be established on a salutary throne. We therefore ask you, students of pure faith and sincere devotion, to present our serenity [Fors. armed with letters], representing us in his presence, since the count is the same from our bones, and flesh taken from flesh, receive him cheerfully and devoutly as a pledge of family love and grace, and in all that pertains to the duty entrusted to him reverently perform to him. and humbly take care to obey with prompt affections, so that the consistency of your devotion to the provision of the august liberality, which knows how to reward the services of the faithful, may be worthily continued in turn, knowing for sure that the signs of obedience which your devotion has shown to him, we shall embrace with equal favor of benevolence, and if it happens to be specially shown to ourselves.

LETTER XXV. *Same with the above argument. (An. Dom. 1275, cod. Rud. XXV.)*

ARGUMENT.--To the magistrates and citizens, as it seems, he commends the same leader singularly to Ravenna, as if he would have his seat in that city, and from there rule the whole region.

LETTERS

To the distinguished and wise men of the elders, consuls, and citizens of the whole world, etc. His grace and good will. While we turn the scrolls of our consciousness, while the states subject to the government, we gaze upon the outstanding examples of pure devotion to our summit in the mirror of royal observation, we turn the line of our mind to your city in particular, which offers us the fruits of faith unblemished. Indeed, how placidly and how gratefully we received, how acceptable, and how generative of the fruitful dance that the native kindness ignited by the breaking spark, which glows in your hearts with a brighter spark of faith, you devoting ourselves to the voice of one command only our messages, which we transmitted to you, so solemnly , and you have received it so honorably, we are certainly unable to express our feelings on this completely by performance. For these are excellent proofs of commendable virtue, these, I say, are sure tests of constancy, and infallible proofs of excellent probity, in which you have hitherto duly rendered to God the things of God, to Caesar the things of his own. Therefore, having been deliciously refreshed by the entertainment of so much sweetness, upon the display of service so grateful and so vengeful, by which you by no means forget the generosity of your forefathers, having acquired a well-pleasing region, we bow to you in the most abundant gratitude, disposing of the aforesaid city (as indelibly by the union of tenacity in our relatives) we have embraced) for this reason to magnify with favors, and to magnify the titles of honors and beneficence, so that at the coming of Caesar, the potentate, who is terrible to the restless rebels, and to you will come meek, driven from the midst of the horrors of the storm of war, whose long calamity has exhausted the face of the empire, calmed in the beauty of peace and rest and wealth, and feel nothing sweeter or more delightful under our yoke of dominion. Moreover, in order that the darkness of your Roman region may be illuminated by the light of the scepter, and that the same region may receive the flourishing growth of innovation, we have taken the opportunity to exhort the prudence of your university to the greatest extent possible, because the noble man H. Count of Fürstemberg, our dearest relative, whom we have made governor of the entire region surrounding you our reverence and that of the government, you will take care to preface it with the insignia of honors; and in those things which regard the general and particular good of us and of the republic, when in the one who is sent, the sender is wont to be honored, and to give favorable advice and timely assistance.

LETTER XXVI. *To a certain prince of Italy concerning the same. (An. Dom. 1275, cod. Rud. XXVI.)*

ARGUMENT.--To a certain prince of Italy (perhaps Napoleon Turriano), who ruled Milan, he thanks him for the singular obedience of having chosen him king of the Romans; praises sincere faith; He promises to show himself royal liberality towards him and his own; and he commends to him again and again the Duke of Furstemberg sent by him to Italy on his advice.

On the one hand, the vigor of your faith was distinguished by which you unceasingly embraced the Roman empire, and in order to increase its honor and beauty with magnificent titles, your soldiers fearlessly shone gloriously among its other tireless athletes and undaunted boxers. This, indeed, among the rest of your magnificences, most agreeable to your royal majesty, appeared to us very gratefully, and greatly applauded our wishes, that, having foretold the arrival of our ambassadors, you immediately withdrew from the enemies, whom they had surrounded with power in a siege, you withdrew the signs of victory, sparing them for the sake of our reverence for the name and honor, which yours it would have been easy for him to have triumphantly submitted to the government. Upon which, in conclusion, bowing to thee in our most abundant gratitude, and commending the excellence of thy faith with a worthy proclamation of praise, we have conceived with an invariable mind to raise thee and thy bountiful gifts of our beneficence, and to enlarge them with suitable honors. Moreover, because of the faithfulness of your plan, under the faith of your promise and your favor, we appointed the illustrious H. count of Furstemberg, our dearest kinsman, as governor of the region of Romaniola and the Maritimes. We most earnestly desire to implore your sincerity, in so far as you earnestly seek to assist him with fruitful advice and timely assistance. Indeed, we wish to earn these things for you and yours with a pleasant and generous turn of events.

LETTER XXVII. *He sends a certain religious ambassador. (An. Dom. 1275, cod. Rud. XXVII.)*

ARGUMENT.--Patent letters to all the magistrates of the Italian states of the Roman Empire, to whom religious N. is granted full royal power to dispose of everything about the same plan for the decorum of the Roman king and the benefit of the empire.

Rudolph, etc. Strenuous, etc. To the distinguished men, marquises, counts, nobles, captains, powers, and commoners appointed by the Roman empire, to whom these letters have reached, their gratitude and good will. By the tenor of the present information of your university, we declare that, having obtained the fullness of the trust of the religious and honorable N. from the circumspection and faith, we have led him to be assigned to the transalpine parts of the empire, giving him a special mandate and plenary power to establish, organize, and procure everything about your plan, which is for the honor of Caesar and the interest of the government seems appropriate. Hence it is that we exhort the prudence of your university with votive affections, inasmuch as, above these things, for ours, and the reverence of the government, aspiring favorably for favorable counsels and aids in regard to the other necessities of this way, and you take care to provide them both willingly and liberally. That for this reason your devotion should be deservedly commended to us.

LETTER XXVIII. *He promised the pope that he would come to Milan for the coronation. (An. Dom. 1276, cod. Rud. XXVIII.)*

ARGUMENT.--By writing these letters to the Roman Pontiff, he gives assurance that he will be present at Milan on the Paschal solemnity, and will proceed thence to Rome to receive the imperial insignia from his hand.

Most holy, etc. That our successful process to receive the diadem of empire from your sacrosanct apostolic hands, wiped off the envelope of every ambiguity, may have the faith of the hearers: see what we promise in good faith, and to this we bind ourselves according to the tenor of the present, that we intend to explain ourselves from all other difficulties whatsoever, in such a way that being present in Milan on the now imminent feast of Resurrection Sunday, from here, according to the good pleasure of the beatitude, we will proceed from the path to the crown of the empire, transmitting to you these open letters of ours as a testimony thereon.

LETTER XXIX. *Rudolph thanks Pope Gregory X for confirming his election. (An Dom. 1275, cod. Caes. 100, cod. Rud. 29.)*

ARGUMENT.--When Rudolph learned that letters had been given to all the princes of Germany by Gregory exhorting them to honorably accompany the king of the Romans, who was coming to receive the imperial insignia, exulting with joy, giving thanks for such kindness, mentioning all the previous benefits, and delaying the distinguished legation for some time on account of A messenger, or a legate known as Probus, precedes the instant of the election.

The beauty of the immense serenity, by the blast of the apostolic trumpet, which had already been showered on all sides on all the worshipers of the orthodox faith, now anew, like the new light of heaven increased by new flashes, pulsating with every shadow of darkness, appeared to us above all from it, and it became evidently clear that the zeal of your beatitude, which directs the righteous causes and detests the unjust, not allowing us to be further attacked by the slanderous insults of rivals, the affection of the father's favor, which he glorified to us by the pious and generous proclamation in the organ and in the equity of justice, mingled with the applause of the sweets, the work of the Most High, which he knit in your person with his wondrous right hand, he brought forth manifestly upon the expression of this kind of favor in public opinion, by sending to our princes and subjects letters of apostolic grace overflowing with the fullness of all benevolence. For which, of course, you have enriched us with inexplicable joy by your bountiful gifts of beneficence, to express our grateful thanks, the tongue of the flesh is not sufficient, since it is not within the power of man to be able to express perfectly by performance the emotion conceived in the mind. O wondrous clemency of paternal piety, which has not disdained to offer us a breast of compassion from the first nascent beginnings of our creation, to stretch out milky breasts sprinkled with liquids, redolence [yielding] a heavy pledge of love! Oh, the ineffable gratitude of the favor, the amazing affection of love, which, long ago in the kingdom, received us sweetly in the arms of education, and fostered between the young [puberty] and adults! Let our intent therefore be alert to this, let our ardent desire continue immovably in this, that above so freely and placidly through you, and the soulful Roman Church, our most pious mother, respond to our progress with the prescient auspices in the reflective filial devotion of worthy decency; However, because for this, as we humbly acknowledge, the possibility given to us is not sufficient, we are forced to implore divine protection, so that from his superabundance of goodness, what is lacking for us, he may accomplish in strength what is pleasing in your eyes to pursue. Moreover, since our solemn messages, which for this and other things that devolve upon us, we have conceived to be destined to the feet of your beatitude, on account of the imminent urgency of our solemn court, which is already to be celebrated in the near future, we have postponed it for a further journey, so that our princes, who are fit there, with a shared plan, the mission to be entrusted will be more famously and festively adorned. Behold, we have entrusted to your holiness the presence of N. Probus, a man whose virtuous actions and powerful works do not conflict with the effect of his surname, to appoint, or even to anticipate, the presence of your sanctity, deposing the most humble requests, in so far as to impress upon them what he has brought to your ears, we gladly hear the same disparage yourself, and anticipate the costs of hearing favorably.

LETTER XXX. *He requests financial assistance from a certain state for the celebration of the imperial elections. (An. Dom. 1275, cod. Rud. 30.)*

THE ARGUMENT.--When the long interregnum, other invaders and others invading, and no one paying the due services of all, had reduced the imperial treasury to the greatest straits, Rudolph, about to hold an election, sought help from the states of the empire.

For a long time I have wavered over the grave fall of the state of the empire, and with the most bitter affection the pressures and groans of the wretched Christian people, that in our happy time the reformed prosperity of the republic may prosper in the growth of a salutary and peaceful repose. . . . . . . Therefore, on such a day, we decided to publish a solemn court at N. Of course, for the magnificent celebration, it is fitting to provide royal equipment. It is true that since we cannot by ourselves be sufficient for the magnitude of the business, and for the support of such great burdens, and the celebration of such a sumptuous festival, we must ask you and our other faithful for a suitable vote and entrust you and themselves with a trustful participation in this kind of behavior. Hence it is that your prudence, with which we can, in exhortations, is most attentively required, inasmuch as, perplexed by such obvious necessity, you care to provide and assist from so many marques, violent and cheerful souls, expressing to you finally by our beloved faithful N., in whose words, We ask you to be credulous, as in ours, to apply the faith that has been decided to be announced to you in our name. Therefore, arises the ever-thankful and laboriously proven readiness of the faithful, which over this the prompt and customary benevolence of well-pleasing royals attaches itself. For in others, we have conceived an unchangeable disposition of mind, so that the antidote of relief, as a change of recompense, will compel your minds, that you will be truly glad, that you have devoted so much gracious obedience to the uses of the Lord. Moreover, your prudence does not ignore the fact that it would be a stain on the indecency of the royal dignity, nor would it yield to your injury, if, which is absent, through a compelling lack of necessary things, you and our other faithful should be troubled with the inconvenience of a pledge for our debts.

LETTER XXXI. *(An. Dom. 1275, cod. Rud. XXXI.)*

ARGUMENT. Rudolph, having threatened by several letters the mind of Henry, duke of Bavaria and elector palatine, who had consented to his election, then turning away the elect, had neglected to ask for a fief, and continued to be obstinate; He threatened him, that he would demand from the electors counsel and justice in the matter no longer to be tolerated.

How, together with the rest of your co-principals, you concurred in our person by a concordant vow, solemnly choosing us to be king of the Romans, how, even afterwards, by a change of purpose, you withdrew from our devotion, turning your back on the royal majesty, and neglecting to demand from us your royal fees, nay, as a probable conjecture He is hanged, despised in pride and abuse, frequently demanded by letters, although sometimes he has sufficed for our free presence to approach you for this reason [Fors. was absent], and we do not believe that the sure possibility has passed from your conscience when it has passed to those who are remote. Because, therefore, without our and the government's mark of dishonor, we cannot conceal your insolence any longer, and we must not, we do not wish to conceal the knowledge of your sincerity, that we have recourse to your same co-principals in vain, of law.

LETTER XXXII. *Rudolph to a certain prince who was attached to the king of Bohemia. (An. Dom. 1275, cod. Rud. xxxii.)*

ARGUMENT.--Writing again in almost the same sentence, he reproaches his obstinacy, seeing that neither letters nor repeated messages could sway him to ask for the investiture of fiefs from his lord; He said to the other princes that such obstinacy was signified, that they themselves should judge of such a crime.

In the fervent zeal of charity, with which we sincerely pursue the universal and individual princes of the sacred empire, like noble members united to their head, to this end sparing no expense, we diligently and opportunely convert, so that by the applause of grateful devotion we are your king, in whom I certainly agree with my wish You will be acknowledged to have consented, as if you were acknowledging the possessor of the empire, and asking us to be invested with your fees. Whereupon we remember that at different times we have sent several suitable mediators and messages to you, and you to us. For we recall that first by N., and secondly by C., our beloved relatives were destined for your presence on the part of the royal majesty, and afterwards in your name, on the contrary, by M. and N., similarly sent to us at different times, the aforesaid business was carried on by various treaties. Indeed, from the meekness bestowed upon us from above, we were presaged, because the placidity presented by the flattering countenance, and the offering of the disguised proposition, which they accepted in pleasant sweetness, produced the event. But far, shame on me! we are separated from our purpose, in vain has he pleased us in the prince, who turns himself more irreverently from the path of our commands. Moreover, since in expectation of this promise the majesty was so royally inclined, that our forbearance in a certain way lost the name of true patience, and the effect, after the same forbearance did not profit, deciding to have recourse to a better remedy, we cannot conceal, nor must we, because of your hardness, lest we should say of obstinacy, the disease of your co-principals, to which extreme necessity really compels us unwillingly, at the right time and place, we will demand judgment and justice for such an excess of the quality of injury.

LETTER XXXIII. *He promises the pope that he will carry out his reformation against the exorbitant bishops of Germany. (An. Dom. 1275, cod. Rud. XXXIII.)*

ARGUMENT.—Rudolph, Gregory X promises that he will use all his efforts and all his strength, so that his decree against the perverted discipline of the bishops of Germany, without the acceptance of persons, is commanded to be executed.

With the ever-increasing growth of the fires of ardent charity, which the paternal affection towards his only son brings forth, as it were, from the hearth already abundantly aflame, our mind is thus infused more widely with a certain relation, and our interiors are more expressively impressed with the benevolent fullness of your favor, to whom your kindness pursues us unceasingly, because from this rising to the praise of the divine song of congratulation, to the gratuitous rededication to the eternal Father, to his holy Church, and not only to you, most blessed father, we are vehemently kindled, and from the power of both men we are desirably aroused all that we are and can be, expounding to your most special nods . Moreover, in your predicable zeal for justice, delighted, as if in the exquisite fragrance of spices, for the fact that the pontiffs who have hitherto been extortionate and who have gone astray have been struck by the sword of due notice, we promise of paternal providence, that if it may happen to any one of them, however connected to us by consanguinity or affinity, who have been rejected by God, and through the mouth of his holy Church, against your commandments to raise the heel of indevotion, in order to destroy his pride, if it pleases your sanctity, we wish to set forth the matter in person.

LETTER XXXIV. Rudolph returns some thanks to the prince for the letter sent and indicates that he has held a conference with the pontiff's family at Lausanne. (An. Dom. 1275, cod. Rud. xxxiv.)

ARGUMENT.--Rudolph writes to his friend the prince, with whom he had exchanged letters, full of joy about the conference held at Lausanne with the Supreme Pontiff Gregory X, and about the appointed day for receiving the imperial insignia in the city from the hand of the same pontiff.

We received your letters which you sent to us with the alacrity of our usual kindness, and in them we surely gathered with our understanding the sweetness of your sincerity. Of course, because their acceptance and the pleasant calmness of our hearts has enriched the interior of our heart with abundant joy, bowing to you for the greatest gratitude for these, we want your desires not to be hidden, because we are going to send our solemn messages to you in the near presence, the faithful interpreters of our purpose, who over our common In accordance with your wishes, they will properly arrange for you, and will inform you more fully and clearly about everything that is convenient and appropriate. Moreover, in order that the continued happiness of our state may gladden your hearts with a certain delicious refreshment, we wish you to perceive with the taste of these, that we and our most holy father, the supreme pontiff, recently celebrated a conference in such a familiar place, by whom indeed in all the affairs of the empire he was received and heard with inexpressible piety. having been more fully heard, on the next present festival of N. we will receive in the city from his sacred hands the glorious diadem of the empire.

LETTER XXXV. *The same argument applies to a certain city. (An. Dom. 1275, cod. Rud. 35.)*

ARGUMENT.--With equal zeal he reminds the imperial city of the same conversation; the soon-to-be coronation of Rome; by which he signifies that ambassadors should be sent from her, that such a solemnity might be duly performed.

That the hearing of your devotion about the fortunate events of our happiness may be gladdened by favorable news, and that the joys of a more fortunate auspices may shine forth, behold, we describe this to you with a clear pen, which we have recently received with paternal affection from our most holy father, the lord Pope N. In the near future we are going to receive in the city from his sacred hands the sacred diadem of the empire. Indeed, since the presence of your messengers there is absolutely necessary to the agenda of such a solemn festival, we encourage and admonish your faithfulness, inasmuch as, according to the request of the honorable man N., you send your messengers industriously and with authority, directed to the aforesaid celebrations of our coronation, so that above all there for the good state of the republic and by the healthful ordering of the Christian faith, you may be more conveniently and perfectly instructed in their relation.

LETTERS

LETTER XXXVI. *Cuida thanks the prince for going ahead of him to Italy to receive the crown of the empire. (An. Dom. 1275, cod. Rud. 36.)*

ARGUMENT.--One of the princes of Germany, who had undertaken a journey to Italy with a magnificent apparatus, and was to attend the coronation, thanked him, promising to return in due time. By the ambassador whom he sends to the pope, he hears a certain day of his arrival, and urges him not to advance, but to continue the rest of the journey with him.

How much he pleased us in the exhibition of your devotion, than now about yours, which does not change, or deviates, we presume from the purity of faith, it is not easy to explain in words or letters. For, out of respect for our honor and sacred empire, abandoning your famous and convenient homes in the fire of crisis, you transported yourself to the parts of Italy with a magnificent equipment in order to march with us to the crown of the empire, we received it very gratefully, bowing to you for this with the most abundant thanks, and to you and Yours, for the time and place, without a doubt, arrange to shower you with so many favors of grace, that you should in no way regret that, for the advancement of our name, you have endured the burdens of labors or expenses. Accordingly, we earnestly require and encourage your sincerity with the affection we can, inasmuch as carefully devising and seeking the most useful ways of our progress to the crown of the empire, do not be weary of our presence, and all yours and others whom you may be able to obey our allurements inductions, it will be known most certainly that in the term which N., whom we have conveyed to the feet of the lord pope, will spread to you more expressively in our name, our desired presence should comfort you and our other faithful.

LETTERS

LETTER XXXVII. *He tries to reconcile the same prince with his brother. (An. Dom. 1275, cod. Rud. 37.)*

ARGUMENT.--Henry the palatine duke of Bavaria, having suffered much, will instruct him, by making a treaty with the king of Bohemia, long ago denounced as an enemy of the empire, to do nothing hostile in the lands of his brother Louis; that Alphonsus, king of Castile, on whose help the enemies of the empire depended, had completely laid aside the title of king of the Romans, and all hope of attaining imperial majesty; that the fraternal reconciliation which he had sought so long in vain would be opportune for him; and lastly, that the king of Bohemia's agreement with Ladislaus should in no way be negotiated by him, lest he himself should be seen as an enemy of the empire.

That the form of your usual salutation is not directed to you by the benevolence of a royal speech proceeding from it, if you choose to balance the treasures of discretion which are placed in your closet of chests with a fair dish and a just weight of judgment, the reasoning is not at all natural. [...] murmuring at your actions, for which reason what is written to others is taken away from you in a dignified way, he is not at all surprised. For behold, illustrious prince, that for your preservation of good state, to reform between you and your brother Louis the solid treaties of peace of old, not without great expense, we interposed our parts in good faith; extermination, and if you have decided well in your own (let us not say any) great progress, you intend to demolish the territories of your said brother, by associating with you the enemy of the sacred empire, H., and his other accomplices, by burnings and robberies, and what is more, not only the prince the loyalist of the government is violently invaded, but the government itself is also hostilely attacked in its own districts. Pay attention, then, illustrious leader, and consider, turn and turn within yourself, be a diligent searcher in the dwelling of your heart, how the command is for you and you are bound together by the command, and the passing shadow does not afflict you [...] it does not linger, so that He will not choose the moment. But that you may clearly understand how some have hitherto tried to circumvent you in your diminution of state, pretending to you the staff of the King of Castile to support you, we do not want to keep you from it any longer, because the said king asserted that he was entitled to all the rights, actions, and questions that belonged to him in the government. , in the hands of the supreme pontiff, he simply resigned, and from the whole imperial dignity, which he had hitherto unlawfully ascribed to himself, he yielded to us in name and in substance, liberally resigning to us, as the true king of the Romans, all that he had up to now claimed as his right in the empire. Wherefore we ask you for royal clemency, in so far as you restrain and restrain your movements, so that you may enable yourself to be well-pleased with the royals, and so that you may see an end in all your actions, that the sacred government will always choose to have a noble member in you as its leader, and you are truly a noble pillar of the government itself. not verbally, you seem to be solidly supporting the emperor's highness. And though we have at other times unsuccessfully engaged in our efforts, that you might be brought back to the fraternal harmony of union with your aforesaid brother, yet he will not be reluctant, provided that you wish to be satisfied in a timely manner, to apply all your care and labor to agreeing. Moreover, since the king of the Bohemians is a manifest enemy of the empire, and continues in the royal proscription, we command you firmly and under the cover of imperial favor, in so far as you do not in any way intrude upon the concord of N. Otherwise, if you should in any way attempt to concur against our restraint, you would appear more clearly to favor our enemies and enemies, and we would not be able to promote and love you as a faithful prince of the sacred empire.

LETTER XXXVIII. *Salzburg promises that he will come to the coronation. (An. Dom. 1275, cod. Rud. XXXVIII.)*

ARGUMENT.--Having received Rudolph's letter, by which he was invited to the coronation, he thought that he was most elated that the priesthood and the kingdom of Syria, in danger of death, agreed to help him by unanimous vote. He would attend the coronation if he was allowed to breathe a little through Ottocarus: otherwise he would intervene with such solemnity through his ambassadors.

Most Serene Lord, etc. Salzburg, etc. A constant servant of devotion and faith in royal letters, the tenor of which he announced to us with full happy sweetness, he made known to us clearly to the next consoled [consoled], and we joyfully gathered from the same, a solemn day, a festival day, that day desired by Rome, from the most holy in Christ our father and established by the lord supreme pontiff, in which the holy mother Church will crown her beloved son, prince and patron, with an imperial diadem, in which the wide breadth of the republic, hitherto narrowed by private abuses, will rejoice, and will see itself expanded again according to the form of its former power under your happy name. In which, finally, the kingdom and the priesthood will sit together under equal purity of mind, so that they can deal with and order when and in what dignified and orderly manner the necessities of the holy land are now, unfortunately, killed by those who are close to them. so that we, who are made partakers of his divinity, may also be mercifully immortal. Therefore, at these sacred festivals, in which the heavens will drop saving dew on the earth, according to our interest, we intend to participate with all our efforts, and hope to rejoice there with the common joys of the Christian people, provided that the frequent and frequently increasing insufferable attacks of your rivals on us will allow us to draw breath and breathe a little. But if, perhaps, by the sins of men, our burden is aggravated by the aforesaid feast of your heaven, we have been unable to honor with our bodily presence, which is absent, we shall discharge the duties of our devotion there with solemn messages, so that we may celebrate that day, which, according to the duty of our name and honor, we cannot decorate, with humble at least we will attend the services.

LETTER XXXIX. *The last letter of Gregory X to the patient Aretius in Thusia to Rodulphus. (An. Dom. 1276, cod. Rud. xxxix.)*

ARGUMENT.--Gregory, suffering from a terminal illness, answers Rudolph's dutiful letters, foreseeing his impending death. He gives him the most salutary admonitions for the best conduct of the prince, and with certain proofs of his love for him, he repeats the turn of love towards the Church of God which he commends to him again and again.

That the height of the imperial summit rejoices everywhere with success, is not a little acceptable to us, since we have always loved and love the honor of your empire and the increase of your happiness so much, that we consider the advantage of your magnificence to be specially ours. In these, therefore, as in the dearest son in Christ, rejoicing in the affections of the father, we remind him of the exaltation in which he predominates, so that, however much the success of human prosperity may smile upon, he should in no way divert the excellence of the internal consideration from the love of the heavenly founder, as well as fear, because without doubt we are brought down by vain delight, if by any means exalted to the pinnacle of worldly sublimity that is transitory let us be entertained by the events of happiness. Nevertheless, to the serenity of your graces we report the actions that, being concerned about our infirmity, you offered us a welcome comfort through imperial letters, and not even undeservedly, because as our conscience answers us, no one can be weakened in the article of this time, or succumb to infirmity, who more sincerely and your happiness and glory it is known more faithfully that he has loved until now. For the very sickness which we suffer, invaded us at that place and time, when, for your honor, whom we have always loved with sincere affection, leaving our country alone, we went to remote regions. Wherefore we are more inclined to encourage thy magnificence in the remembrance of this kind of love, inasmuch as we set all these things before our eyes in pious meditation of the mind, and redeeming a good turn for us, whether God rescues us from the labor of this infirmity, or brings us up from the prison of bodily frailty, always love and honor his Church; and as the most pious prince and the most Christian emperor, endeavor to bring him peace and rest, so that whether we live or die, in his presence, we may glory in your good works, to whom even in this present life we attend as the debt of our servitude, and to whom we boast of his mercy. if he chooses to summon us, we will proceed with confidence.

LETTER XL. *He writes something in the Roman court and clears himself of the suspicion of the left. (An. Dom. 1275, cod. Rud. XL.)*

ARGUMENT.--Rudolph of Lausanne, who was always treated liberally by Master Bernard (I am not mistaken, the treasurer of the holy see), when a cloud was once caught on his forehead, worried about the delegated religious man, and added the most dutiful letters, excused himself, not even realizing that he had injured him.

Rudolph, etc. To the honorable and wise man Master Bernardo. The serene calmness of your gentle countenance, representing the mystic of the heart, representing the indication of the royal actions until now, not ignorant, not fearful, and encouraging of our virtuous instincts, so warmed towards us, so strongly prevailed, that with the exception of our most holy father, the lord pope, we principally ascribe to you, not undeservedly, everything of honor, and To the progress of our sublimation of glory he added the right hand of the apostolic consolation. For with the utmost confidence, we have revealed to you all the innermost things of our mind, to you [Fors. upon your] shoulders the weight of all care and concern, from which indeed the longed-for benefit proceeded and the longed-for advance came forth. But again, which we report with a heavy heart, it has seemed to us, by certain remarkable conjectures, that towards us that praiseworthy serenity of your countenance has probably changed, and the gentleness of your mind has been sharpened, upon which the inmost thorn of wonder has deservedly struck, perplexed by the unexpected novelty of this matter. . For the witness is the untainted truth of the conscience, more solemn than any deposition of witnesses, that nothing has ever been attempted by us in word or deed, or even in thought, that should have given birth to a spirit of displeasure to you. , with the appropriateness of the season to offer himself, to be present with gracious and ample favors, and to aspire more abundantly to the affluents of our beneficence. Now these things (however our movement may be founded at the beginning) we submit securely to your discretion, according to which your providential inspection may please, to be freely decided. It is for this reason that we earnestly request your honesty, in so far as you are willing to receive our apology with a meek mind, and to sweep from the sanctuary of your mind whatever mist or evil impression of left suspicion may have suggested, with the broom of right opinion, by introducing the charitable guest of truth. And behold, for this reason we have specially appointed an honorable and pious man to be appointed to you, earnestly asking you to take care to place unquestioning faith in him, as the truthful promulgator of our innocence.

LETTER XLI. *Answer to the preceding letter. (An. Dom. 1276, cod. Rud. 41.)*

ARGUMENT.--Bernard, on the contrary, had perhaps provided occasion for suspicion, that he himself had not visited Lausanne, a region not unknown to

LETTERS

the county with a multitude of business, and that he had been obliged to remain there long after the retirement of both courts. In the rest, he deserves praise rather than suspicion of his genius; that he was, and would be, unchangeable by the ingratitudes of those who blocked him. He would not add anything to the death of the pontiff but would announce the election of his successor.

In the letters which your excellency has lately addressed to me, the eye was horrified at the complaint formed by my change towards you, and the mind, not without great astonishment, discussed more attentively, searched more carefully, what could have formed the origin of this complaint, what change, which the truth certainly does not know to be disordered, perhaps He gave even the faintest hints of the fancies of each one, and what kind of conjecture he offered. In these doubtless scrutinizers the scrutiny failed, the opinion of the discussion found nothing: for how could it find that which was not? For if the intention of his complaint is referred to the things which had been done at Lausanne, it would by no means be tolerated by the exacting labors in arranging your affairs, unless, perhaps, some occasion for controversies arises from the fact that I did not come personally to your presence in the hospitality of your dwelling at that time, as the Most High knows of those same affairs occupation, which, as you know, detained me there after the departure of both courts, did not permit. If, however, those things which were committed to the venerable father N., and which afterwards by the merchants, by special command, fel. Rec. Sir Gregory, through my letters to some of your relatives, I opened the same way that they are directed, the very quality of their deeds, which rather awaited the herald of merit than any imposture of changeability, to protect innocence. Moreover, illustrious prince, there is no need to dwell on excuses, when, as a witness, who is a faithful witness in heaven, no instinct of accusation can even be conjured, which perhaps some detractor intending to harm both you and me has formed in a third language. Concerning this, therefore, let the concern of the royal highness rest, because mine, so that my speech may be known without boasting, constancy known by the grace of God, and from every variety until now removed from infamy, has hitherto persisted unmoved, and while the vital spirit nourished the frame, under the auspices of God, unaltered, solid and unblemished it persists. Of course, among the others contacting you, a full conference was held with N., and he writes to you more fully as we have agreed together. Regarding the calling of the mentioned father, the present letter has been deliberately withheld, because since it is a pain to remember pain, I did not think that your hearts should be inflamed by the repetition of the removal of it, but that it should be sweetened by the sanctity and justice of the substitute.

LETTER XLII. *To the cardinals, after the death of Gregory X, that they may choose a good pontiff. (An. Dom. 1276, cod. Rud. XLII.)*

ARGUMENT.--Rudolph, having received the unfortunate news, while he was setting out to receive the imperial diadem, stopped, and wrote to the sacred college of cardinals, bringing forth many and true praises of the dead pontiff, whose funeral he said should be followed by the whole world and especially with his own tears, by whom he was exalted above all kings and with paternal love he had been beloved. Hoping that a successor will be chosen who will complete the work begun, they are begged to choose the best successor as soon as possible, who, according to their decrees, will be bestowed with imperial insignia on the solemn day. He would not continue his journey without their or the future pontiff's deliberation.

From the garden of the militant Church, the gardener of the fore-marked was transferred to the ecclesiastical mansions. They sing peaceful sermons to God, yet the earthly crowd of the faithful mourns for his departure. Let Greece, then, bewail the desolate propitiation of her convert, for the drachma which had been lost for a long time has been rediscovered by her gift [number], and the sheep which had long wandered through the desert of indevotion, joined to the flock by Dominic, are now fed by him with salutary pastures. The Latins bring up sobbing sighs from the depths, whose manners the same father of virtue directed in the path of salvation. Moreover, let all the tribes of the earth mourn and howl upon themselves for the taking away of their faithful father, but most of all those who, assuming the victorious sign of the living cross, under the safe leadership of the same father, managed to rise up powerfully against the blasphemous enemies of the Christian name. Let this common weeping go forth into all the earth and let the pain of lamentation reach the ends of this world, because the setting of so great a Father has brought down the tears of many, who watered some more abundantly by the example of happiness. Nevertheless, among all the other kings and princes of the whole earth, especially with the feeling of compassion, our eyes languished for want, already dried up in abundance of tears, because the same most holy father, setting up our throne above kings and kingdoms, while he lived, comforted us with his pious embraces, and packed us with paternal favor. Moreover, when human resources and skill fail to repair this expense, which is rather comforted by the providence of the heavenly disposition, and not by the general equality of fate, the remedy for the same pain, the marks of which will scarcely ever pass from our breast to the scars of the dead, we, from strength of spirit, in this we have offered to ourselves in the hope of undoubted confidence having conceived that he who did not allow his chosen servant Moses to lead the people, will substitute another in his place, not unequal to the brightness of his merits, that he will consummate everything successfully, healthily ordered by the aforesaid holy father in the zeal of God. To this end we beseech you, pious fathers, fervent hinges and pillars of the universal Church, exercise vigils, and apply dutiful cares and labors, so that, relegated to the obstacle of every contention, the necessary prince may be erected more quickly in the acephalous world, where the divine instinct will prompt you and the weights of equity may be subjected. For the rest, it is possible, as it is read and known by infallible arguments, that one generation perishes, and the next succeeding generation, because nevertheless the earth stands firm for eternity, that is to say, the Church of the living God continues unmoved in its actions, and in the ordinances of actions prepared by a mature deliberation [about it and that], before of the death of the aforesaid most holy father, a hostile and cloudy rumor had reached us, we had properly girded ourselves and our people for the journey, so that according to what had been arranged by your mediation, if the fates had favored us, we might have received from his hands the diadem of the most sacred empire. But although it may have been seen differently in the Most High among the founder of all things, who will arrange in the apostolic seat a man according to our own heart, as we believe; still, however, in the very purpose of our proceeding, prepared together and girded, persevering unmoved, and hoping for the invariability of the mother Church, we suspend the journey itself for a moment, and relax for a time, until through you or the future supreme pontiff, whose good pleasure we always intend to obey in all things with the readiness of the spirit, we shall more perfectly It happened to be informed what was now to be done for the devoted son of the Church.

THE SECOND BOOK.

FIRST LETTER. *Rudolph congratulates Pope Innocent V on his election as Roman Pontiff. (An. Dom. 1276, cod. Rud. I).*

ARGUMENT.--Rudolphus, in the same opinion, and in almost the same words as he used in the previous letter to the sacred college of cardinals, congratulates the new pope-elect Innocent V. He praises him with great praise, submits himself to him as his only son, and says that, in accordance with Gregory's determination, the imperial diadem is in his hands, God thus disposing, he will accept. He sends Henry, bishop of Basel, his speaker, both about the coronation and about other matters to be done with him.

The heavens rejoice and the earth exults in the voice of festive delight; for there are celebrated festivals of the Catholic faith; there are new joys after the lamentations of the sacrosanct mother Church; for the Lord, who sometimes turns away serenity from his bride, in order to turn again to her in the brightness of a greater joy, did not cut off his mercy from her own, the face of the Church, any more than in death. Rec. Lord Gregory X, the supreme pontiff of our most blessed and most gracious father, had covered the mourner with a cloud of sorrow, shining a ray of successive consolation, and multiplying him as always with a new fetus, raising up a new father for the deceased, conspicuous by the brightness of his merits, and luminous by the excellence of his virtues, by whose delightful effect of substitution whatever a flood of grief burst into his cheek, for he was suddenly lifted up, it is hoped, doubtless, to be wiped away. And although our eyes have languished because of the poverty of our father, because of the poverty of our eyes, which have already dried up in plenty of tears, because, besides many other glorious and preachable things, which he conceived and established for the good state of the Catholic orthodox faith, establishing our throne over kings and kingdoms, while he lived, the pious he supported him with his embraces and extended his paternal favors; from that, however, the signs of our sadness, the scars of which will hardly ever pass from our chest, we have already proposed to ourselves a remedy, that he who did not allow his chosen servant Moses to lead the people, placed a man according to our heart in the apostolic seat, who, adhering to the footsteps of his most holy predecessor, everything should be completed successfully by the same predecessor and healthily ordered. Moreover, as each generation passes, and another generation succeeds it, the earth stands still forever, that is to say, the Church of the living God perseveres in its actions, and the ordinances of the actions, having been prepared by a mature deliberation, immovable, as the evidence of works has taught. For this reason, most blessed father, from whose divinely ordained creation our spirit has completely revived, fertilized with an ineffable dance, we beseech you to gather into the bosom of your grace an only son of yours and of the well-pleased mother of the Church, that he may always be born in all the readiness of the spirit, kindly completing the work of God in us by the power handed down to you from above . Indeed, it is probable that we cannot think that the consummation of such an arduous task is reserved for you by the heavenly glory, that he may complete it at your right hand, whose gracious protection he did not feel himself to have experienced from the beginning of our sublimation. Behold, then, he would come. Brother Henry, bishop of Basil, etc., to you and to the Roman Church, devoted to your beatitude, we have most faithfully laid them at the feet of your beatitude, beseeching them with devoted devotion, that you may give him a favorable hearing to whom we have poured out the inmost parts of our hearts, and that in all our actions you may condescend to exercise a credulous faith, as we do , the hearing [from the hearing] subsequent costs.

LETTER II. *Rudolph writes to the cardinal after the death of Gregory X, pontiff. max., and commends his legate to him. (An. Dom. 1276, cod. Rud. II.)*

ARGUMENT.--On the same occasion the sacred college of cardinals admonishes them to send themselves to the new pontiff, and at the same time to send an orator to them; that he had appointed the bishop of Basel, who would be freed from his affairs, and he commended him to all.

Having changed, as it pleased the Lord, the state of the sacrosanct mother Church unexpectedly in these days, in whose change so sudden ours could not be established, without bearing with it the inconveniences of the change. Behold what came. No. to whom all the secrets of our hearts have been communicated, like an imaginary of our presence at the feet of the apostolic beatitude, and we have led it to you in confidence, asking more attentively, and exhorting you, inasmuch as we set forth his speech overall and each of you, that you take care to apply the same credulous faith to us, to their campaign, gratuitous help and effort, as we trust in your kindness, effectively applying.

LETTER III. *He rejoiced at the newly elected pontiff and appointed him procurator in the Roman court. (An. Dom. 1277, cod. Rud. III.)*

ARGUMENT.--By this royal decree he appointed a new procurator, or his legate at the holy see, with the necessary powers. He instructs him about the things to be done and promises rewards for the same good deeds.

God, the exalter of the lowly, foreseeing our desires from on high, he foresaw the husband of the desires of his holy Church as a suitable bridegroom, and if anything, if we dare to say, he existed imperfectly in his predecessors, as if through a complete form he has mercifully deigned to complete in our most holy father, the pope. Indeed, in him our soul rests, in him we place the anchor of our hope, that he may rule with us in the kingdom, command in government, order, and arrange the things which are the salvation of both men. Moreover, we believe, nay, we are certain, that you must be with him our eye not sleeping, our ear open, our right hand directing and guiding our deeds; so that our direction and advancement in the Holy Roman Empire should yield to you and yours from generation to generation to the exaltation of name and honor. Moreover, with our most holy father, we have appointed you as our agent to consult and to obtain by persuasive persuasions everything that will benefit the holy Roman Empire, not contrary to the most holy wishes, but in all things agreeable to him, for his own will not at any time differ from ours willy-nilly. Watch for us, fulfill your ministry, complete the work of a faithful man, and prepare for the rest of us the crown [care] of justice.

LETTER IV. *Pope Innocent commends the Cologne church and archbishop to Rudolph the emperor. (An. Dom. 1276, cod. Rud. IV.)*

ARGUMENT.--Innocent V Siffridus, the archbishop of Cologne, as well as his Church, bearing the distresses and injuries of his Church with a most unjust heart, commends them both again and again to the king of the Romans.

Innocent, etc. Dearest son Rudolph in Christ. We recommend the churches and ecclesiastical persons to you the more faithfully because we know that you have a more prompt zeal for them, and through which you render acceptable obedience to God and render yourself deservedly favorable [most favorable] to men. Of course, as we have received, the noble G., Count of Julias, not content with the fact that he had long ago affected the Cologne Church with serious injuries and pressures, he still visited the Church itself. He would not be afraid to afflict our brother bishop of Cologne with innumerable hardships and various persecutions. But because we trust that by the help of your favor the same Church, which we are jealous of with paternal affection, will breathe from its own distresses, we affectionately beseech and exhort your highness, inasmuch as having the aforesaid archbishop and church more willingly commended for divine and our reverence, assist them in their rights, and defend them with the divine power entrusted to you; in such a way that you deserve the divine propitiation the more abundantly, and we can commend your devotion with merit.

LETTER V. *He congratulates the pontiff on his new pontifical dignity, commending himself to him in submission. (An. Dom. 1276, cod. Rud. V.)*

ARGUMENT.--Rudolph is about to move his camp into Austria against Ottocar, King of Bohemia, and he hastily writes back and congratulates the new Pope John XXI, to whom he promises to send suitable and solemn messages at a more convenient time. Meanwhile he submits himself and all his people to the pontifical will: and finally, he warns him of the expedition to be immediately undertaken against Ottocar.

Most holy, etc. Laudable and glorious in eternal ages, the son of God, blessed and blessing all who trust in him, the inscrutable organizer of the eternal and the transitory, comforted the holy mother Church with the bounties of the most abundant consolation, he deigned to anoint her with the oil of joy, to place the anointed in a safe station. When you have been divinely elevated to the summit of the highest dignity and the most holy degree of apostolate, indeed for the reformation of the empire and the salvation of the Holy Land, reddened with the precious blood of Christ, the same holy Mother Church, renewed with the joys of renewed joy, congratulates you with the exultations of votive fruitfulness. No wonder: For the God of peace and love, of immense goodness, has set in his very signs, when he appointed you a father to himself, he has mercifully chosen you as a shepherd of his flock. The matter of this immense delight, even if it should move all who recognize themselves as members adhering to the head, we rejoice first and foremost in your exaltation, the more clearly, we know that we have been called to the desired salvation by your infinite goodness, and by your supporting counsel and help. This testimony of him who is the searcher of hearts and minds, we cannot so much explain in letters or messages as we carry in our hearts and in our minds. From so much mercy, therefore, as we have conceived of your holiness, without any doubt of deliberation or consultation, we surrender our own person, spouse, children, sons and daughters, possessions and honors held and held by your holiness's hands and orders, reclining the head of our humility in the bosom of your mercy , that we may truly say with the wise: I have sought rest in all things, and I will dwell in the inheritance of the Lord; we will dwell securely, who cast all our care upon you, because we know that you care for us. How then shall we turn from your ways? and shall we depart a little from the way of your commandments? we submit everything to you, we deliver everything into your hands, we want to live with you and have you as ruler in the kingdom, so that between us there is an identity of minds and an inseparable union of wills. In these few, most holy father, we have decided to express the joy of our mind by means of a secret and familiar message under a certain haste, visiting the presence of your holiness with continuous after this suitable and solemn messages. Moreover, we desire to know your holiness, that by the divine clemency favoring us, the princes of our entire Roman kingdom stand favorably for us for the recovery of the property, rights, and goods of the empire, and with their advice, strength, and support we are strongly girded to defeat the infamous man king of Bohemia, ours and the holy Romans the only insulting despiser of government, the possessor of many principalities, hoping in his mercy, who resists the proud, but gives grace to the lowly, that we should accomplish our purpose in praise of him.

LETTERS

LETTER VI. *Rudolph writes back to the king of Hungary and apologizes for not having accepted his prayers. (An. Dom. 1276, cod. Rud. VI.)*

ARGUMENT.--Ladislaus, being asked by the king of Hungary as his chamberlain, some districts in the lands occupied by the right of Ottokar, replaces, as the law of the lands being still uncertain, it would be less expedient to grant anything in them; .

Having received with kind affection your royal letters of late addressed to us, and having read and more fully understood them as it was fitting, we have decided to answer your highness in this manner upon a series of them. Although we would like to be vengeful to all that can soften your mind and affection, and although we embrace with open arms the respectable man N. your chamberlain, for his illustrious and virtuous merits, with open arms of gracious benevolence, because nevertheless we ourselves, and our beloved princes N. and N in certain lands, which the infamous king of Bohemia is allowed to occupy, we contend that we have the right, it seems no less reprehensible, if so suddenly, so precipitously, to the collation of certain districts pertaining to the same lands, without such a declaration, or discretion, to whom it is to be known, or to whom by right if they were competent, it would happen to us to jump; therefore your extended request to us for the said N. is for the present frustrated in effect, which certainly does not disturb the royal mind with a spirit of displeasure, since, as you know, the process of doing things of this kind must be balanced with balanced judgments, and with mature examination plans, and exact, so as not to be subject to changeability and inconstancy I was charged with the main presidency. Nevertheless, in order to raise the titles of your glory, we bear so fervently the feeling of unshaken sincerity, that whatever pleases you and us above this, in the singularly abundant affluence of benevolence, as much as we can freely and liberally aspire to injury without right.

LETTER VII. *Rudolph promises that he will take revenge for the crime committed. (An. Dom. 1275, cod. Rud. VII.)*

ARGUMENT.--He admonishes the prince who adheres to him by faith in the writing of Ottocar's defects or distrust, as he was then dying, that he should continue to denounce him as an enemy of the empire; announces the hostilities of a certain Ottocar adherent; the abomination admitted in the priest is detested.

By the example of a terrible and destructive thing, which has recently reached our ears from the cutting of a certain priest's vessel in the seminary, announcing to you, we are prepared with a bitter feeling of pity, ready to enter into the correction of the committed crime at will. On the distrust of the king of Bohemia, as you wrote, thinking more deliberately, that it was captured at a more suitable time, when it was decided against him the sentence expressed, so that the process is completely devoid of slander, the distrust itself is celebrated. Moreover, in order that the rumors which we have recently received may not be hidden from you, we describe to your sincerity that N., in favor of N., again entered a certain city with several chariots and horsemen by force, exterminating it by burning and plundering.

LETTER VIII. *The archbishop of Saltzburg accuses Rudolph Caesar of being his suffragan, the bishop of Sequoia. (An. Dom. 1275, cod. Rud. VIII.)*

ARGUMENT.--Frederick the archbishop of Salzburg, who, running with Conrad of Frisingen into Styria and Carinthia, and being brought over by his suffragan Bernard of Secco, as if he were to raise up the people subject to Ottocar to defection, had been compelled to consult him in flight; He accuses him of the delegation to the Augustan elections, of boasting against the government and the holy see, and of subverting the clergy and the people. And he begs him to observe the insolence of one as an example to others.

Lord, let it be known that our suffragan bishop of Secovi, forbidding us and unwillingly, undertakes missions contrary to God and to you, in defiance of the devotion of the Roman Church, which he owes to you and to us. While the same bishop had recently passed by us, we fraternally and secretly rebuked him for this; but he himself, by our correction, has recklessly blasphemed against us, and come. our brother Conrad bursting forth into foolish talk, publicly proclaimed it to many great men present, and said that we had both descended to the lands of his lord the king for no other reason than to treacherously disturb their state in your favor; and he provoked so many supporters and accomplices of his party against us, that we were obliged to flee from those countries by perverse roads, with great reproach to our name. The same bishop about certain foolish words in narrow, boasting of himself, not only withdraws and diverts the laity from your devotion, but also incites clerics and religious men, and suggests that they rebel not only against the government, but also against the apostolic see. Our plan, therefore, which we join in the prayers, is this, that you should consider with all your effort, how the said bishop, who alone raises himself up among the suffragists and other prelates, and extorts, and gives others an opportunity of offending, having shown by the effect of the penal work how reckless he is To injure the Roman majesty. For we know that if you fasten the cheekbones of his reckless mouth, the hands and lips of others who rise up foolishly from the opposite side will also rest.

LETTERS

LETTER IX. *The gravest complaint of the archbishop of Salzburg against Ottokar, king of Bohemia, after the death of Gregory X, pontiff. max. (An dom. 1276, cod. Rud. IX.)*

ARGUMENT.--Ottocar, after the death of Gregory X., loosening the reins of his anger against those who adhered to Rudolph, put the bishopric in such straits. He threw out Salzburg, so that he was forced to implore royal protection. Wherefore he sends a messenger who tells all evil things with his mouth; moreover, he informs Rudolph of the creation of a new pontiff, and of his future coronation, and promises to continue in faith towards him constantly in all dangers.

To his most serene master of Salzburg, the most ready with devout prayers for any well-pleasing will. Those who defiantly raised themselves against the holy Roman Church and the sacred Roman Empire with the horns of their rebellion, which had long been shaken, after the death of our most blessed father and lord Pope Gregory, exulting in the worst things, so outrageously and audaciously, as if both dignity and power, which we believe to be immortal by the grace of God, be destroyed by the death of one man. It is easy, but pitifully [wonderful] to see this in us and our church, who for that alone suffer persecution, endure reproaches, and await our own extermination, because we willingly spend the servitude owed and devoted both to the apostolic see and to the Roman Empire; to whom we recognize that we are bound to the obedience of fidelity, as the bearer of the present, who knows well our innumerable distresses, will fully recite to the royal sublimity. whom we also specially sent to see the royal glory, that he might investigate with sagacity and skill the matter of the creation of the supreme pontiff, and of your process, which we desire to make our state more prosperous, which we do not stand, but slip; to bring forth a plan, the protection of which is to be directed among our distresses, the weight and number of which are increasing day by day, in this perilous time. For in this purpose of our deliberation the constancy of our decision is steadfastly and inviolably established, so that it may not be destroyed by the weight of any adversity, or by the storm of any danger, but that our faith may be more apparent and shine around you and the Roman Empire. Therefore, may it please your majesty, prince and glorious lord, to be comforted by the sound advice of your information, our misery, the end and number of which we do not see, according to what the bearer of the present will explain to your ears.

LETTER X. *Again, the Bishop of Salzburg made a more serious complaint to Rudolph about Ottocar, King of Bohemia, from whose tyranny he begged to deliver himself and his people. (An. Dom. 1276, cod. Rud. X.)*

ARGUMENT. He cries out for help: he writes that his constancy was not tested by anything; they would rather die themselves and their people than fail from the government; He went to great lengths to bring some of the weak from miserable servitude; He asks Rudolph to come as soon as possible, to redeem those provinces and rule over them.

To his most serene master, etc. of Salzburg with the prayers of untiring devotion of faith. Thus far I waited for him who would make me safe, being placed in distress, exposed to death, and dying every day for justice, you, lord savior, impulses and verses frequently that I should fall; I was solicited many times to bring against you the apostates of the faith and the deserters of the truth. I, indeed, trampled down by the fierce fury of men, through no fault of my own, and forsaken by almost all my dearest, and held in derision, did not deny thee my lord; I suffered insults and terrors from my acquaintances and relatives because of you, I lost myself and my family by fire and sword, in order to make a profit and save others who, departing from the devotion of the government, sold themselves into miserable servitude at the price of their [precious] blood. May your soul live, sir, may it live and be strong, may it come and not tarry, so that we may not see death; his [whose] fear is next, indeed to me and to those men of the strongest heart and faith, who, for zeal for justice, for the laws of empire, have chosen, like the other Maccabees, either to triumph with you in a glorious struggle, or for you, if necessary, to rest in an honorable death rather graves, than living to await innumerable calamities every day, and finally to die a dirty and ignoble death. Indeed, I attracted those whom I could, I comforted the weak, I strengthened the small-minded, and in faith I supported the majority until just now, so that nothing remains for you but to come, take the kingdom, and return. What more can I say? Whatever may happen, whatever face of fortune, which varies the fortunes of men, may show itself now serene, now turbulent, yet my faith will never fail in regard to you and the Roman empire. For either I will bring you into my province the redeemer of the afflicted people with jubilation, or else I will flee and not see the face of the persecutor. Send us news of happy news.

LETTER XI. *The same Salzburger sends his correspondent to Rudolph Caesar and urges him again and again to arm himself as soon as possible for the deliverance of himself and his people. (An. Dom. 1276, cod. Rud. XI.)*

ARGUMENT.--Thirdly, pouring out more effusive prayers, he sends his reporter, which he used to drag the people to his submission, to tell everything clearly. To dwell in the utmost speed of the matter, lest continued affliction bring despair, despair bring defeat. Everything was ready for victory; Rudolph's name was formidable to those who averted it, to bring triumphs. He advises him to take care of his life, and to beware of the snares of his new friends.

My dear Sir, whatever I have hitherto directed with those men concerning you and their affairs, I have carried out almost all this through the service of that man's reporter. The works of truth commend and prove his diligence, as great as he was. I send him now to you, that from his own words, and other certain indications, which he will show you, and the frequency of my labors, and the purpose of those men gathered together, you may take care to look out for you more than [themselves], considering how much danger of their lives they are under by your grace. submit They waver between hope and fear, and may the despair which your delay might induce, not sink the confidence of those poor afflicted people. Whatever has been neglected this summer will hardly recover from the rest. Behold, because for your sake they leave everything and empty themselves, what then will become of them? Be to them a tower of strength in the face of the enemy. I hold this as certain and true, that all and every one who will come to you and have come, will gladly enter with you, and will undergo the danger of death for you, nor will they deny you if it is necessary for them to die with you; for this, that the torments of flesh and spirit, in which they die daily in themselves and their dearest servants, may end together [end] the agony; I believe that the matter of the rest is an easy one, and a well-arranged opportunity to conquer it, if I choose to conquer it. I see the countenances and hearts of those who oppose you so trembling and cast down with fear, so destitute of strength, that those who fear not yet knowing you, not yet seeing you seen, flee from the face of the bow, and shudder at the sound of your name. What will they do, and how will they be afraid of the voice of thunder, when the eagles come upon them like flashing lightning? The giver of the present has well earned, and will still earn more, that in his pious and just petitions he may find grace and favor in your eyes. Be the watchful guardian and loving provider of your life. You are protected from the scheming of those who sometimes surround your side. There are many who persecute and trouble me, but before my life fails my faith, I will not turn away from your testimonies, in which I have set the law and the end [faith].

LETTERS

LETTER XII. *Rudolph replies to the bishop of Salzburg, thanking him for his extraordinary care and vigilance about him. (An. Dom. 1276, cod. Rud. XII.)*

ARGUMENT.--Rudolphus trinis archiep. Salzburg. He replies to the previous letter from the camp held after the election of Campidunus, thanking him most for the sincerity and constancy of his speech and actions. He alludes to Ottocari's cunning and says that he committed himself to publishing the rest of the letters by word of mouth.

Upon the uncontaminated fervor of your friendship, which is so pure and whole, which you bring to us with the promptest zeal of mind, we do not seek foreign evidence of words, where the effect of the work outweighed by the said one, clears up certain experiences for us, and our witness conscience interrupts more solemnly by any deposition of witnesses. We know indeed, as we have proved in the following list, that in your preconceptions towards us they do not remain, but the more they slip in time, the more gracefully they grow. This, of course, is more clearly evident to all from the contents of your letters sent to us. From the tenor of which we judge a probable conjecture, that by watching over our sides you exercise the duty of a watchman and fulfill the business of the royal guards both healthily and faithfully, since nothing can meet us so stormy, so cloudy, and so impervious to light, and opaque, without being calmed by the command of your luminous prudence. Therefore, upon these salutary admonitions of yours and the free reformation with which you have usefully prepared us, paying thanks and gratitude to your fatherhood, and for these and other sweet indications of your goodness and will, exposing us and ours to any of your gestures, of the events of our prosperity, which we are pleased to hear we believe you, we have led these things to be published by your wishes. That our court solemnly celebrated in such a place and on such a day, with a large company of princes sitting before us, and a retinue of pre-chosen militia, the like of which has hardly been seen in our times, we celebrated it in a manner fitting for the potentate of the region, with appropriate constitutions issued to a number of people, decorated with military belts with many soldiers, and with all the other things which magnify the king sitting on the throne, and exorcise the royal court, having been properly conducted, and omitting nothing of the contingent, although the cunning of the sitting king of Bohemia from the north has been seen in secret, since he was unable to oppose in public our so famous advances, and the intention of such profitable and festive solemnities [in temptation] evil contraries; which [he] who, however, by the right hand of the Lord doing prowess, failed in his cunning, did not make progress. As for the rest, our beloved family [servant] N., the exhibitor of the present, will explain more clearly with the oracle of a living voice.

LETTER XIII. *The same complaint was made to the emperor Rudolph of Salzburg against a certain count about the violent occupation of the monastery of St. Paul in Carinthia. (An. Dom. 1279, cod. Rud. XIII.)*

ARGUMENT.--The same archbishop relates that, while he was in Patavia, having performed his province, it was reported that a sacrilege had been committed by Count N. in the monastery of St. Paul in Carinthia. Of course, N. had been chosen as his suffragan, and had been brought from thence to the castle of N., looking at him, and had been extorted from the same prisoner by the count's force and fear. This kind of sacrilege must be rectified by the same count, so that those lands may no longer be subject to the ban, and that all the prelates, unpunished for such a crime, should be subjected to such atrocities: which he expounds again and again in the name of all.

To his most serene master, etc. Salzburg's constant and faithful purpose of serving. We have recently settled at Patavius in your province, and a sad accident occurred in Carinthia, which we report to your royal majesty with grave complaint and sorrow. Count N. de P., after having performed and transmitted the sacrament to you and to the government, sent his spicules into the field. the monastery of St. Paul in Carinthia, who, with the noise and shock of their weapons, entering the same monastery, presumed to drag the captive lord N. out of the monastery with bloody hands, and led him bound to a certain fortress of N., which the same elect held in his power, and while required by them He delayed surrendering our camp to them, they prostrated him to the ground, and having put their bare swords three times to his neck, and inflicting other corporal and grievous injuries, he surrendered our camp to the same count himself in fear of imminent death, having been carried away by him in the same camp with much food and many other valuable things. And although the province of Salzburg, at the time of the persecution, was disturbed by many troubles in its clergy, yet it never endured so terrible an injury, at the gross indignity of which all and every one of the inhabitants of our parts are justly amazed and afraid with astonishment. And unless this recent and bloody temerity is avenged by the royal power, many others will rise up, who, like the aforesaid count, will trample underfoot the state of the clergy and the churches. We beseech your royal majesty, then, in the name of all the prelates of our province, in so far as the said count, who, with diabolical presumption, violated the double sanctity of the Lord in a sacred place and a consecrated person; and who, disregarding the homage due to us, took possession of our castle both by deceitful intrigues and open insults, for the excess of this committed by Lord N. Count at the time of the crime committed, and still established in those parts to be made such amends as to satisfy both our and the whole clerical order's injury. and other clerics and prelates, expecting similar events, will not despair of your protection, while it also comes to ours. the persons of the bishop of Chimen (whose same count is a carnal brother) who thus perseveringly adhered to you, and were the first of the others, may see this wickedness perpetrated with impunity. It is also necessary for your piety to meet the crime committed so much, lest the lands, which have been subject to the ecclesiastical interdict from the statute of the provincial council of ours held a long time ago, may long be deprived of the divine, and lest the people, who still waver in doubt, go astray in error and scandal, which is easily done if he can, he will be abducted. But woe to that man through whom this stumbling block comes. Prohibited also because of the form of the statute, which we have long since done for fear of the Lord King of Bohemia, as N. and N. bishops fully know, we neither dare nor can we relax, unless the injury is first retracted, which Count M., if he wishes, will be able to fully reform. We are also for the present set on a journey, by which we enter Carinthia and Styria for the increase of your honor, and thence descend to the parts of Austria.

LETTER XIV. *The patriarch of Aquileia writes to Rudolph the emperor about many things, especially about the king of Bohemia. (An. Dom. 1276, cod. Rud. XIV.)*

ARGUMENT.--Raymund Turrianus, patriarch of Aquileia, writes to Rudolph in a letter that he rejoices that he adheres to the faith and plans of the Turrians, and brings war to King Ottocar of Bohemia. Against him, hostile to himself and his Church, he promises help. He would have no disagreement with N., however, lest he destroy the castle recently erected against the rights and privileges of his church. He will immediately return to his church, so that he will be ready and ready to serve it.

Most serenely, etc. of Aquilegia The royal counsels, which require examples and signs of pure faith and prompt devotion, I accepted with more prompt honor, and having read them with the most affectionate feeling, I conceived such immense joy that the spirit, the mind, and even the senses, were each renewed with joy. Indeed, it is a matter of great delight and exultation for me, that the royal highness, trusting in my faithful faith and mine, chooses to conduct the Caesarian proceedings according to our plan, as if it were more salutary offered to him, and to the king. It is also a specially overflowing heap of joys for me, that your imperial serenity has graced the throne with virtuous works, which befit the glory of such a master, and managed to decorate your despisers, who, like the pillars and bases of the empire, should run with all readiness in the way of your commands, under the right hand of your power he intends to humiliate, and to trample down with the hammer of dejection, with the exacting demands of rebellion: so that he who is at once calm in his precepts is looked down upon, angry with revenge afterwards, and whom the faithful of all and every one, who represent the debt due to your excellency's fidelity, know a sweet and pious master, into confusion let their rivals feel their own corrector. For the more recklessness to be punished is increased by excesses, the greater is the correction to be applied to the offenders, so that they themselves may at least know their deed by avenging punishment, and others may be restrained from unlawful punishment by the fear of vengeance. Moreover, since the mind of the writer is so fixated on the promotion of your exaltation, that the sum of my desires is chiefly to procure the honor of your honor and name by word and deed, I desire to know your magnificence, that I must gather my power with men and forces, so as soon as possible about your successful process against the king Bohemia (who, contrary to God and all justice to my rights and to the rights of my church, exists as an injury and a dishonor to honors) has stood up to me, I will render myself prepared for the services of your excellency. The rest of your letters had a favorable introduction, so that I endeavored to arrange myself for a settlement with N. Upon which I thus explain by those present my will, that between me and him there is not at present any matter of dissension or rancor, nor will any scruple of discord arise from me concerning him; that the integrity of friendship and love may flourish and flourish between us. Nevertheless, it is that he himself, being in your service, caused me to erect a certain fortress to the prejudice of my church, and against its privileges and public law, which, unless perhaps he himself, choosing the path of equity and justice, desisted from injuries of this kind so undue and violent, could have been inductive of malice, and more than expedient, nutritious. For the rest, although in these parts, instead of directing your steps, and preparing your processes, I had prolonged my stay until now, behold, I hasten to return to my land in an instant, that I may be able to render myself more ready and ready to serve you, according to the burning desire of my heart.

LETTER XV. *Of the captain of Styria, who, under the name of Ottocar, king of Bohemia, laid waste all the goods of the Church of Salzburg; he writes the same to Rudolph of Salzburg, asking him for speedy help. (An. Dom. 1275, cod. Rud. XV.)*

ARGUMENT.--Archbishop. He announces to Rudolph of Salzburg that in Austria, Carinthia, and Styria, all are hostile to Ottocar persecuting whoever is faithful to the king of the Romans; and lastly, that he had sent troops into the church of Salzburg, which they had almost destroyed by robbery and murder; the enemy was willing to be appeased by no other agreement than by abandoning the faith of the church and the government. He asks for speedy help from him, so that the little that remains is not corrupted.

The indignation which the Lord King of Bohemia has unworthily conceived against the church of Salzburg, as we have learned by experience, will not rest until we and the trace of our church are obliterated from the earth. For after all had perished in Austria, Styria, and Carinthia who worshiped justice, and the laws of the Roman empire had been obeyed, after our faithful devotion could not be removed or changed, having been tempted by many terrors, by various false promises, and solicited by the aforesaid king with more flatteries. Behold, on that day the captain of Styria, in the name of the aforesaid king, invaded all the estates, squares, camps, and towns of the church of Salzburg with a hostile army, and captured men, and killed most of them, and carried off the movables, but the immovables were so cruelly devastated by fire and sword, that already of all his nothing is seen of the said church surviving, which has not been trampled upon by enemies. And although we prostrated ourselves with devout humility and begged the grace of peace, or at least the inducements of a truce, from the same king, yet we agreed to accomplish these things on no certain condition, unless we wished to become infidels against the Roman Church, and the sacred Roman Empire by the rash debt of our faith. We, therefore, in our straits for the veneration of Augustus, implore help and await the support of your most fortunate majesty, beseeching with sorrow and groaning, so far as at least the remains of the said church have been miserably abandoned, lest that very thin and little resource, which fell from the claws of the robbers, be absorbed again by the same, by hastening to the aid of the vote, before it happens to us that we shall be completely consumed.

LETTER XVI. *Rudolph writes to the nobles of the kingdom of Hungary that he will soon take revenge on their enemy the king of Bohemia. (An. Dom. 1276, cod. Rud. XVI.)*

ARGUMENT.--Rudolph praises the nobles of Hungary for their faith and concern for the youths, King Ladislaus and Duke Andrew, who were adopted by him as sons; and, having confirmed what he had done, he enticed them to claim honors in the Roman kingdom, or in the court, affirming that it was his heart to restore the former glory of his kingdom, and to rival the audacity of Ottocar, God forbid, to break.

That the vigor of your unfettered faith and the grace of natural power illuminate, that the invariable strength of your mind shone a glowing spark of purity, appeared by the bright evidence of works and became clear by real documents, while the illustrious Louis king of Hungary and Andrew, duke of Sclavonia, our dearest sons, bereft of paternal consolation by the fate of human fatality (whom as flesh from our flesh, and bone as it were from our bones with the embrace and bosom of our father, we assumed to be cherished) without ceasing to anticipate services, and to adhere to them in their own and kingdom's actions with dutiful and unceasing embraces. Upon which of your laudable acts, in which we seem to have been pleased, as if in a delightful repast, we pursue your studies with the most abundant returns of thanks, and we applaud you with laudable commendations. Desiring, therefore, to abound towards you more affluently in reality than in words, we ask for a special gift, inasmuch as if any prerogatives of this kind shine forth in the Roman kingdom or among us, that your mind may be gladdened by these, as you require them from us with the confidence of obtaining them. For it is beyond doubt that we have the heart and care to direct that magnificent and famous kingdom of Hungary by a reformation that restores the bundles of its ancient glory, and thus to destroy the ferocity of that persecutor by the very injury that we propose to avoid absolutely no loss of persons or things, but to destroy the same proud pride under the victorious eagles , the leader of the Lord of hosts, let us consider: that he learns in a good way, by placing an eyebrow by himself, how hard and how difficult it is to kick against a spur.

LETTER XVII. *The emperor Rudolph commends his eldest son, whom he sends to Austria with military forces, one to the prince, to help him in everything. (An. Dom. 1276, cod. Rud. XVII.)*

ARGUMENT.--Moving the camp towards Egram, and having sent Albert the eldest into Austria with a strong army, he asks the same from N. to march through his own territories, promising that there will be no trouble for the places or the people, and asks him to order the peoples subject to him to be the protection of the same Albert, that is, the yoke that Ottocar had imposed upon them a long time ago.

Rudolphus, etc., Our peace of mind is not undeservedly disturbed, and we are stirred up to anger more violently, and as much more justly as you and the other princes and faithful of the sacred empire, because of the purity of the faith which you carry to the Roman empire, we are more severely afflicted by the rabid tyranny of the illustrious king of Bohemia. Indeed, we intend to show the manifold affection and affection which our serenity bears towards you, caring for you with fervent and unrelenting desires, to you and to the rest of our unjustly afflicted princes, likewise and oppressed, by a laborious and speedy succor and support of the mighty, and in our vow we bear towards Aegram together with his son L., the king of kings, directing our steps with success, to assist us in hasty progress, our first-born towards the parts of Austria, with a great number of armed men and an abundance of armed soldiers, with the most decent equipment. Since it is necessary for him to cross your borders without the injury, expense, or loss of any human being, we ask that you endeavor to prepare for him away and an entrance for our first-born, according to which we have unshakable confidence in your fidelity and discretion; making and arranging that your faithful should support the same from their fortifications, nay, themselves, and that they should pursue their business in supporting our first-born so ardently and so energetically, that having thrown off the yoke of servitude imposed upon them by the aforesaid king a short time ago, they would be able to breathe in the quiet comfort of peace. We commit our said son to the purity of your faith, and to the counsel of your examined discretion, and, as if for a son, we hand you over to be instructed, governed, and directed in all that pertains to the liberation of the country.

LETTER XVIII. *Rudolphus, the emperor of the duke, signifies that he will move against Bohemia and occupy the neighboring camps. (An. Dom. 1276, cod. Rud. XVIII.)*

ARGUMENT.--In order to prepare a safer course for himself against the king of Bohemia, N. urges him to occupy the camp of his enemy as far as he can, bordering on his domain. The prize promises praise and honors.

How by cunning tricks, how by attacks of slanderous intention, the reckless enemy of the empire of N. contrives for the disinheritance of the same empire, is enough, as we believe, to be known to you in your neighborhood, which has already passed to the distant ones. Of course, when, in order to recover the splendid possessions of the empire hitherto occupied by him, and to raise the standards of the imperial power in the near future, under the supreme leader of the Lord of hosts, we arrange to exhort your sincerity, in which we have no small amount of confidence, by the most extensive instance by which we can exhort the kingdom, in so far as the occupation of the camps of the aforesaid king, which are closer to your power, [Fors. provinces], do not fail to turn all the cares and studies of your mind to the opportune times, so that a freer passage may be open to us for his invasion through the same places, and a more convenient entrance may be prepared for us and ours for the perpetual extermination of his desolation. For by this means you and your contemporaries will doubtless be prevented by the announcements of our magnificence and be exalted with noble honors.

LETTER XIX. *Rudolph Caesar apologizes to the Roman Pontiff for not coming at the appointed time to receive the crown of the empire. (An. Dom. 1275, cod. Rud. XIX.)*

ARGUMENT.--Rudolphus protested to Gregory X that after the conference of Lausanne he had nothing more ancient than undertaking a magnificent apparatus for the Italian journey to the imperial coronation on the holy day of

Pentecost, as had been arranged; but for some time he was hindered by serious affairs, which his ambassador will relate.

He, most blessed father, was incessantly exuberant in his zeal for carrying out the well-pleasing mysteries of his father; indeed, he will constantly bring forth in his breast the effects of filial devotion, to pursue the ministry of the mother Church with honorable worship, because just as it happened that we were departed from your beloved presence, we spared no costly labors at all, but were decently girded with regional equipment for the journey we hoped to embark on in the end for us by your kindness, from your sacrosanct hands the diadem of empire. But the success of this kind of process was not absent [Fors. was present]. Nay, and the tangled conglomeration of unexpected accidents which befell afterwards, somewhat restrained the prompt spirit from the execution of such a noble work. These troublesome obstacles to your sanctity we have decided to discuss rather by the speech of a faithful interpreter than by writing. For this reason we most faithfully destine a religious and honorable man, N., conspicuous for his faith and devotion, shining in the purity of his life, and accepted by us by the clear merits of his honesty, into whose mouth we have poured our words upon the foregoing and others perfectly, at the feet of your beatitude, that he may report cases of this kind. , humbly beseeching him, that he would condescend to exercise credulous faith upon them, as upon ourselves.

LETTER XX. *He stirs up Ladislaus, king of Hungary, and Andrew, duke of Sclavonia, against the king of Bohemia. (An. Dom. 1276, cod. Rud. XX.)*

ARGUMENT.—Rudolph Ladislaus, king of Hungary, and his brothers Andrew, duke of Sclavonia, as if adopted as sons, and united with him by treaty, announces that he will deliver them and their kingdom from the tyranny of Ottocar; He commands them to be of a high and great spirit: indeed, they are to fight with an equal and fortunate prince.

The connection of a placid parentage, which unites us in the embraces of an alternate identity, is thus implanted in our fore-hearts, thus indeed has it firmly rooted and firmly rooted, and constantly coalesces, implanted in the plants of our memory, which, among the rest, whose frequent concern affects us, is most strongly attached to our wishes, such as you and Inclytus N., whom we have embraced as flesh from our flesh, and as bone from our bones, and cherished in our paternal bosom, we may rescue from the furious tyranny of the unjust persecutor, and enlarge the cords of your ancestral heritage to appropriate ends. For it is undoubtedly our heart and concern to direct that magnificent and famous kingdom of Hungary by reforming it into the bundles of ancient glory, and thus to destroy the ferocity of that persecutor with the very injury that we propose to avoid absolutely no loss of persons or property, except to tame the same proud pride under the victorious eagles. Let us focus on the leader of the Lord of hosts. So that he learns in a good way, by raising an eyebrow by himself, how hard it is and how difficult it is to kick against a spur. Here, then, is the prince, in whom the noble energy of our ancestors has spread the strength and courage of free derivation, put on a virtuous man, girding you with the strength of courage. But we trust in divine clemency, that you will not lack a good outcome in all things, as long as you are fighting in an easy and fair cause, and under a fortunate prince zealous for justice.

LETTER XXI. *Rudolph invites the commander of the army to the service. (An. Dom. 1276, cod. Rud. XXI.)*

ARGUMENT.--The commander, with a part of the forces sent forth to recover the provinces of the government, praises him for the excellent deeds he has done; and he announces to him that he will soon proceed to Austria with a magnificent apparatus, and that the royal bounty will follow him.

It is sufficiently open and well-known to the royal highness, how much virtue there is in you, how clear and calm it shines with evidences and well-known arguments, how much purity of energy and faith shines, while thirsting and greedy for our glory, not avoiding the expenditure of persons and things, to leap to the exaltation of the empire fearless, you do not stop, gloriously and energetically directing the troops of our army entrusted to you. Upon which, of course, we recommend the achievement of your consistency, which was satisfied in the exhibition of the work. Of course, we do not wish to ignore your wishes, because in the near future, under God's guidance, we intend to present ourselves to the parts of Austria in a powerful country and with a magnificent equipment, worthy of being liberally provided with benefactions for your merits, and in accordance with the plan of your industry to provide for the end of a salutary business.

LETTER XXII. *Frederick, the archbishop of Salzburg, absolved his diocesans from the oath they had taken to a certain prince. (An. Dom. 1276, cod. Rud. XXII.)*

ARGUMENT.--The archbishop of Salzburg absolves his provincials from the oath of allegiance by which they were bound to the King of Bohemia; and on the advice of the suffragans he threatens to strike with anathema any one who does not adhere to Rudolph after obtaining his oath.

Frederick, by the grace of God, etc., the fullness of all good things with salvation. Since the holy religion of swearing is not a bond of iniquity, but rather a confirmation of the truth, prudent and provident men, of whom we count you among the number, fully understand and easily grasp that the sacraments administered to the illustrious prince N. by you and others against the sacred government, and your master Most serene, they neither hold nor bind you, because they have been unduly twisted against the leader and justice and the state of the republic. and since the same oaths cannot be observed without prejudice to your safety and mortal danger to your souls, we, by the authority of Almighty God, release and absolve ourselves from you, nay, let us declare that we are not bound to observe them. We will also discuss the plan. By the sentence of excommunication of our suffragans, we will proceed against each and every one who, under the pretext of the oaths thus taken, have chosen to wander in the wayward conception of error, rather than be brought back to the path of open truth, which the Roman Empire has already led us before God.

LETTER XXIII. *Rudolph writes to the king of Hungary for help against Bohemia. (An. Dom. 1278, cod. Rud. XXIII.)*

ARGUMENT.--Rudolph of Vienna, having already been stationed since the retreat of Ottocar, and gathering help from all sides against the same rebel, and then preparing for the last conflict, begs the king of the Hungarians to give him protection in the duchies of Austria and Styria, so that if the enemy turns, he may pursue him from He reminds the king that he has established himself in the rear.

When alliances of kinship and friendship are sometimes contracted between the kings of the world and the princes of the world, the greater the union of affection between them must be born with merit, the more the greater must set others in higher mirrors of dignities, the inferiors must discuss the examples of virtue, and the more through their unanimous wills peace grows firmer among the peoples, it is enlarged the honors of each other, and of their own, are strengthened for posterity, and the rights of the kingdoms. Of course, the identity of the alternate connection successfully contracted between us for a long time is so truly inextinguishably rooted in our hearts, so tenaciously established in the innermost affections of our hearts, that it pleases us to carry out by effect whatever softens your royal spirit, whatever we would think to be attractive to your majesty's honors, with an unchanging mind disposing, to observe the bond of this bond indissolubly. Hence it is that, reciprocating from you the debt of the inviolable friendship thus contracted between us, according to which your agent and messenger is acknowledged to have pledged, and to this solemnly bound you, we ask for the royal serenity as much as we can, with the greater affection of the country, and we encourage each other in our needs aided by aid, and to our faithful and supporters in the leadership of Austria and Styria, who are pretending to be an effective patronage shelter and a support of comforting advice and help, as our beloved faithful NN have led His Royal Highness to inform. For we in our city of Vienna, in order that the king of Bohemia might be able to sufficiently repulse the king of Bohemia, we contracted a useful delay in this turn, so that if the aforesaid king should perhaps direct his rash attacks to the attrition of our own loyalists, following him manfully in the rear, the same king, who was said to our loyalists, let us be able to strike We beg you, therefore, to write to us with haste, what is going on in your purpose upon the premises, and what is contained in your good pleasure.

LETTER XXIV. *Rudolph accepts someone's apology, so much so that he does not want to be the mediator of peace between himself and the King of Bohemia. (An. Dom. 1276, cod. Rud. XXIV.)*

LETTERS

ARGUMENT.--The excellent prince responds most liberally to the supplication of Bernard, bishop of Seccovia. He denies that he will accept an arbiter of peace between himself and Ottocar, unless Ottocar first makes good the immense damages inflicted on the bishops.

We received your letters sent to us at last with kind affection, that they might reveal the veils of shame, which the zeal which the priority of your letters had discriminated and scattered, rendering you harmless. It is true that the royal highness has never until now disbelieved in the infallibility of your rectitude, but whatever artifice a man of a pure heart could have infused into you of a ministering nature, he always considered that it was divinely given to you. From these, then, which sincere rusty hearts not susceptible of scars, have probably already brought to light the excellence of your famous opinion, and commending the steadfastness of your constancy with worthy praise, we gladly admit your apology, and approve the shining titles of innocence. Let those who, ignorant of the truth, dictate to you empty pamphlets, see what honor and glory they derive from such comments. Furthermore, on top of what you have written among the rest of our highness, you are willing to interpose your parts for the good of the concord between us and the King of Bohemia by means of an anxious mediator, so we have decided to answer you. That when the same king extended to our princes, archbishops and bishops, as it were to the apple of our eyes, both hands of hostile invasion, severely debauchering their continuous extermination, we think it utterly incongruous and unbecoming, so fiercely and fiercely, that we were wrapped up in the envelope of negotiations and doubts. It is true that if he would withdraw his hand from offending, and correct the wrongs done by restoring those who have been taken away, we could be more easily inclined to those things which would be appropriate to reason.

LETTER XXV. *Rudolph urges his cousin to go with him against the King of Bohemia. (An. Dom. 1276, cod. Rud. XXV.)*

ARGUMENT.--He exhorts a prince or count of his blood to help him against King Ottocarus of Bohemia, promising him with great rewards and benefactions that he and his family will pursue him for his merits.

Of the union of noble blood by which you are bound to us, thinking that you would in no way degenerate, your sincerity, in which we trust with no doubting faith, we have taken the greatest instance we can to exhort the precum, inasmuch as the natural stretch is the cord of parentage by which we are joined, worthy considering that the auspices of royal sublimity attributed to us are yours divinely , and the perpetual increase and magnificent support of your excellent posterity, strive for us and our supporters in the moment of emergency, against the unjust power of the invader, to assist as manfully and constantly, and to defend us faithfully against those who attack us. Indeed, in this case, your case is treated as undoubtedly as ours. Wherefore, if thou art prompt in thy heart to do what is desired, the royal highness will magnify thee and thy kindred with honors, and indeed will enlarge the favors of his fruitful beneficence.

LETTER XXVI. *Rudolph conveys to the prince a certain office in the government, and invites him to join in the war, and through him others. (An. Dom. 1276, cod. Rud. XXVI.)*

ARGUMENT.--A blood relative of another prince in the province of Ottocar, exposed to the throat, confers the duty of the empire to be recognized by the princes, when he approaches the imperial court. In the meantime, he commends to him constancy in the faith, and earnestly begs him to entice his uncles to the same, with the hope of rewards.

We do not hesitate to supply you with a double incentive, which is so ministering to us and to the Roman Empire, that you serve us, as argumentative bees. Therefore, manly men, whom neither flattery subverts, nor does adversity frighten, commending constancy with praiseworthy of proclamation, and disposing of an unchangeable spirit, we are worthy to magnify you, like a distinguished seal placed in our hearts, with honors worthy to be magnified, and to exalt with suitable honors, we describe to your faithfulness that office No. We commit to you even to the good pleasure of our will. For we have confirmed by oath that we cannot alienate the imperial goods without the advice of the princes; , but even in the more fruitful comforts of our beneficence you should be deservedly honored. Moreover, when the noble N. has thus withdrawn from our presence, that he, together with his others, should rise up powerfully against the enemies of the Roman empire, and openly vouchsafe to you a patronage, as from him and his coadjutors, if you convey your messages to them, you will be able to be more fully educated. We earnestly demand and encourage your sincerity, inasmuch as, not letting your mind be swayed by any impression of fear, and being guarded by providence from the snares of those who lie in wait, you may persevere manfully in the purpose which you have begun. Your uncles, on whom we wish to shower a rich influx of rewards in the same way, to assist us, etc., in the business itself, will be effectually enticed by the inductions you can; for we have conceived to lavish the sweetness of our beneficence on you as well as on themselves in such a way, that you will efficiently forget your labors, with the abundance of the coming sweetness of the rewards.

LETTERS

LETTER XXVII. *Rudolph congratulates a certain prince on the agreement entered into and incites him against Bohemia. (An. Dom. 1276, cod. Rud. XXVII.)*

ARGUMENT.--Rudolph congratulates Henry, duke of Bavaria, who had been reconciled with the best of the public with Louis, his brother, the count palatine, and begs him to send back news of the marriage celebrated with Otto, his own son, and the royal daughter; He attacked Ottocarus from his side, who he himself attacked from the other, so that he could not escape between the two fires.

He has brought into our heart a great matter of exultation, which, by the already quiescent spirit of swelling, which the crash of the terrible storm had brought between you and the stricken bridegroom of our daughter, by the disposition of his clemency, which gives clearness after a cloud, in the same way you are united in the votive reconciliation in a kiss and fraternal sweetness, which of course, like you to glory, so he will yield to faithful subjects for the increase of the desired rest. It is true that a cause of astonishment is infused into our hearts, that our messages, which we have long conveyed to your presence, upon the conclusion of the marriage, have contracted such a long and protracted delay in your court, which we indeed ask to be finally disposed of. And because our faithful in Austria are shaken by the insults of a fierce enemy, and are attacked by bitter attempts of persecution, we implore your calmness, in which we trust with a steadfast faith, to the greatest extent possible, in order that you may endeavor to attack their invaders from that side as manfully and powerfully. For we, trusting in the finger of God, who attends and directs the justice of our cause, we will try to attack and conquer them from this side in such a way, with the power of the Germans, that the aforesaid invaders will be led between the hammer and the anvil by the penance of the perpetrators. In this way, you will not only be able to recover the boundaries taken by your ancestors, but you will be able to extend them to larger cords. Therefore, if it pleases you, as soon as you have seen those present, you will intimate to us more clearly what is going on about these things in your purpose and is contained in your good pleasure.

LETTER XXVIII. *Rudolph writes something about the defection of the Carinthians from Ottokar, King of Bohemia. (An. Dom. 1276, cod. Rud. XXVIII.)*

ARGUMENT.--Meinhardus, apparently endeavoring to bring the people of Carinthia to his submission, announces that they have come to him from the borders of his province, N. and N., and having asked for pardon, they have withdrawn at once to declare war on Ottocarus, and to invade the places in the same borders. He thought that he should share this with his followers, so that they might become more active.

Having lately come to the presence of our majesty NN and having held a careful negotiation with them in the form of this information, they simply departed from us, because, immediately distrusting the king of Bohemia, they would extend their hands of invasion against him about the borders of Carinthia and would vigorously attempt warlike assaults on NN and NN on our submissions. in the same border with heart and mind, and with work, as it is probably believed, applying. Say these things, then, and command the faithful, whom you think will be glad of our fortunate auspices, that as they are eager for our honors, so they may be congratulated on the share of our glory, and that they may be stricken with fear and trust in the arm of the Augustus to protect themselves against the attacks of slanderers and the snares of their rivals.

LETTERS

LETTER XXIX. *The archbishop of Salzburg and his suffragans joyfully announce to the supreme Roman pontiff, through Rudolph the emperor, whose virtues and praises they extol wonderfully, that Austria has been freed from the tyranny of Ottokar the Bohemian. (An. Dom. 1276, cod. Rud. XXIX.)*

ARGUMENT.--The archbishop of Salzburg and the suffragans, after Rudolph's first victory over Ottokar, king of Bohemia, congratulating John XXI on his election as the new pontiff, exaggerating the tyranny and audacity of the same king, recalling to himself and all the other bishops from the council of Lyons, which he had evidently exercised, withholding tithes for relief of the holy lands, obedience to the commands of the holy see, and obedience to the king of the Romans confirmed by apostolic authority: nor unlawfully by extorting oaths, subverting churches by burning and plundering, and entering into an alliance with the tyrants of the Tartars. From time to time Rudolph's most fortunate progress, having been very richly recounted for the liberation of Austria, only the king, as well as the republic and the churches, commend him for his merits with gratitude.

Most holy, etc., such bishops, etc. Raising our hands to heaven, we joyfully sing praises to our redeemer, the Son of God, Jesus Christ, and we humbly bow down to the gratitude of his extraordinary piety, who, invoking the prayers of his holy Church, placed your most holy paternity in a towering mirror, so that it shines from on high, and shines like a bright pearl enlighten the minds of the Christian people. At this same happy time, in which the divine grace revealed, the blessed Peter, the prince of the apostles, the apostolic father, deserved to ascend to the leadership, the Son of God, blessed for ages, visited his people in the parts of Germany and raised the horn of salvation for us. Indeed, the Lord lifted up the horns of the righteous at this time, and broke the horns of the sinners, which were specially raised against the body of the whole Church to be corrupted and carried to our death. And although many, as we believe, were the narrators of this matter before your clemency, we nevertheless reveal to your fatherhood the sequence and order of the truth of what happened to those present. Having lately returned to our own country from the council of Lyons, and desiring to carry out those things which had been healthily ordained in the council itself, the illustrious Ottokar, king of Bohemia, summoned us to his presence, and expressly forbade us to collect the tithe assigned to the support of the Holy Land in his territories, nor any He would preach the glory of our saving cross. He also demanded that we should be careful, by swearing and other different precautions, that neither at the command of the apostolic see, nor under the pretext of issuing a sentence or command from any man, should we do anything that would deviate from his purpose; by which he determined to resist the Holy Apostolic See and the Roman Empire fiercely, not only from us, but also from the inferiors of any of the superiors of our parties, exacting, through fearful fear, illicit oaths. On us, who did not want to be defiled by this crime, he imposed the harsh yoke of servitude, and with a fixed mind he finally decided to destroy our innocence, using exquisite tortures and cannons. And although the accumulation of so many evils had sufficed for our extermination, from this fear the aforesaid king made us utterly lifeless, because he united himself by a league of alliance with the tyrants and kings of the Tartars. Hearing these our miseries and the injuries of Christ, the Christian prince, and our dear lord Rudolph, the most serene king of the Romans, and hearing our often-heard prayers, assembled with the strength of a military army, moved his camp from the uttermost borders of Germany, passing through long distances of the earth and various nations, about the feast of all saints. he entered the districts of the Austrian land, not fearing the precipitous peaks of the mountains, not abhorring the weather of the winter season, nor abandoning [lack of] the deep snows of the frozen region. After the principality of Austria, Styria, etc., had triumphed with triumphal glory, the city of Vienna, among the best of our parts, which the king of Bohemia still held in his power, surrounded him with a large army, with ships nevertheless wonderfully arranged in warlike equipment, with which he arranged to cross the broad river of the Danube, as aforesaid the king of Bohemia, who was already thinking about the protection of his flight, would occupy the heart of Bohemia, as if he were a fugitive. But the said king of

Bohemia being healthy indeed, but relying on slow counsel, asked for a truce of a few days, and obtained what was requested, under which the army came to the aforesaid Lord [Rudolphi], and there present to us, indeed broken in spirit and bowed at the knees. He obtained the devoutly requested pardon, having previously resigned all the hostages, states, camps, and towns which belonged to the said principalities. But the lands of Bohemia and Moravia deserved to be invested with a tribute of fidelity. Therefore, we commend this glorious prince to your sanctity, most pious father, supplicating humbly and [not so humbly as] devoutly, inasmuch as, for God's sake, you deign to have the aforesaid lord recommitted to you, in whose hands in these days, according to evident signs, divine justice triumphantly triumphed.

LETTER XXX. *Rudolph praises the king of Hungary for the war he undertook with him against the king of Bohemia (An. Dom. 1278, cod. Rud. xxx.)*

ARGUMENT.--When Ladislaus, king of Hungary, had opportunely enlisted the help of his side, Rudolph, rejoicing with joy, poured himself out in extraordinary praises, abundant thanks, and ample promises. He adorns him with an insignificant message, which he will receive from him, if he pleases.

To the illustrious and magnificent prince Lord L., etc., the affection of paternal sweetness with safety. Oh, how glorious, what a remarkable foreshadowing of future joy! Oh, how great, how excellent a sign of virtue has been given to our hearts about a son so illustrious, so high above the kings of the earth, who gradually ascends to the heights of honesty, strives in his tender and early years to be adorned with the insignia of the manners of his years, and to be clothed with the wife of a grown-up man. Of course, how immense, how inexplicable the matter of exultation has poured into our hearts, that to avenge our and your injuries, which are united by certain individual ties, against the common enemy of the Roman empire and the kingdom of Hungary, you have raised your power so powerfully and magnanimously, it is not enough to denigrate the tongue, or the writer draw a pen worthy of condescension. For this reason, raising our organ to the divine praises of the heralds, we bow our gratitude and thanks to your royal highness as abundantly as we can, promising greatly that no adversity of hostility will ever be able in any way to bend the indissociable alliances made with you, unless we regard your cause in all things as properly our own. Behold, therefore, we transmit our solemn messages to your presence from our side, that they may deal with you providentially and order how we and you may proceed more magnificently and more deliberately; which, however, we leave entirely to your disposition, at whose nod we have committed our desires; to be sent with the campaign costs.

LETTER XXXI. *Rudolph refers to certain conditions of the treaty entered into between him and the king of Hungary. (An. Dom. 1277, cod. Rud. XXXI.)*

ARGUMENT.--Rudolph states how at last a treaty was entered into by himself with Ladislaus, king of the Hungarians, which had long been begun by ambassadors sent to and fro, then ratified by public letters, and finally, by the joint right of both contracting parties, at the place of the sacrament, it had been absolved. And he narrates the conditions of the same, especially those who entered against the king of the Bohemians.

The arranger of good counsel and the arranger of right wills has so uniformly agreed upon us with the magnificent prince Lord L., that the other of us esteems the fact of focusing on the other's losses and gains, advantages and disadvantages, and deems it to be his special interest. Recently, having agreed with us, and looking on with joy at the vision of N., all and each promises or ordinances begun here and there by our councilors at different times, and finally approved by open letters from both of us, we both kings were equally appointed approved and approved, and we promised to keep forever, given the faith one to the other manually, in which turn and place we performed the sacrament. We have also added this of our common will, that in disputes and questions concerning damages given and injuries inflicted, or any other that we have against the illustrious king of Bohemia, one will help the other as faithfully as manfully, and never without the good pleasure of the other and the agreement with the aforesaid king break the peace. or he will celebrate harmony; nor will he have a treaty about them, to which we bound ourselves under the pledge of the same faith. As for the rest of the boundaries of our lands being legally distinguished and kept distinct in peace and harmony, we have decided to arrange them in this way, etc.

LETTER XXXII. *Rudolph informs a certain prince of the remarkable victory obtained by the king of Bohemia. (An. Dom. 1278, cod. Rud. xxxii.)*

ARGUMENT.--Let him inform his friend the prince of the remarkable victory which he and the united king of the Hungarians had won over Ottocar, with the slaughter of Ottocar and most of the Bohemian nobility. Only the triumph over the most powerful enemy is reported to God, whose clemency he had been rescued in the extreme danger of death. To him and to the blessed Virgin Mary, thanks must be given.

With how many insults and insults, the unceasing disturber of the republic, once the illustrious Ottokar, King of Bohemia, pushed us to raise the hand of our power to check his nefarious attempts, no one knows you better, no one saw more clearly than you, dearest prince, who the conspiracies which the same king had made against our salvation , you are not ignorant of the darts of ambush which he had tried, the snares which he had hid. And since at one time you received with us the snares of bitterness, the drafts of furs, from the torrent of such a crisis, we believe it worthy that you should be happily satisfied even now, rejoicing at our triumphal victory, after you have perceived the quality of what we have accomplished from these letters of ours. Know, then, that on the Thursday next after the feast of the blessed Bartholomew the Apostle, we pitched our camp in that place, where we were scarcely distant from the tents of the said King of Bohemia to the distance of half a Teutonic mile. But on the morning of the following Friday, marching together with our beloved son, the King of Hungary, we attached the wedges of our spears to the enemy's station, and so at about the sixth hour of the day a serious battle began between us, in which the said king of Bohemia, defending himself manfully as a vigorous fighter, at last fell defeated and died. He was not prostrated by our own power, but rather attacked God by suddenly attacking the republic. In which war the nobles of the kingdom of Bohemia either fell dead by the sword, or were defeated in the battle, and while they turned to the protection of flight, they were detained by the pursuers. But since it is clear to us from true and certain evidence that it was not ours, but the power of the most high God, who mercifully protected our life, that triumphed in such a crisis, we ascribe the present glorious victory to the title and honor of him, who, to end the distresses of our humility, then mercifully inclined the merciful eyes of his immense clemency. while the danger of extreme necessity threatened. You, therefore, most dear prince, give thanks to the Most High, and turn your heart to the praises of the glorious Virgin Mary, by whose protection our life stood safe at the point of death, and the honor of the Roman Empire, pitifully bowed down, breathed in wonderful strength.

LETTER XXXIII. *The same Rudolph signifies the same victory to the Roman high pontiff. (An Dom. 1278, cod. Rud. XXXIII.)*

LETTERS

ARGUMENT.--Nicolaus III., declaring the same remarkable victory to the supreme pontiff, carefully discusses the perjury of the king of the Bohemians, and the certain causes of this extreme conflict, and a certain principle.

We believe that the apostolic sanctity would be threatened by any event that ended that suit, in which the once illustrious king of Bohemia, tireless tirer of the republic, and the notorious persecutor of our safety and life, raised himself against us and the Roman Empire imprudently, after the sacraments of fidelity and homage which had been granted to us and which he had badly despised. For the said king, on the feast of Pentecost which had just passed, moving his camp against the lands of the empire, and subjecting them to the desolation of plunder and fire, made a hostile attack on certain camps and towns. By pushing us with so many damaging insults, and slanderous insults, and contempt, that in order to defend the state of the republic, the foundations of which the same king had almost destroyed, it was necessary, at least late, to bring forth the power of the sword entrusted to us by God. Thus, on the morrow of blessed Bartholomew, we and our son Louis, king of Hungary, encamped in that place, where we were scarcely a Teutonic thousand miles distant from the army of the King of Bohemia. But on the morning of the following Friday, invoking the help of the eternal God, we proceeded, and with the belligerent standards raised, we arrived at the place where the King of Bohemia was arrayed in battle, and awaited the end of the battle. There the soldiers of both, while looking at the signals from one side to the other, cluster together in a fierce attack, and there the equality of forces is debated between us with drawn swords. So great was the feeling of triumph on the part of each party, that everyone esteemed it a worthy and due thing to procure victory by death, and to live by dying. There the soldiers are trampled down by the hooves of their gallant horses, and there the earth is drenched with so much human blood, that not only those who fight, but also those who look upon the severity of the battle, might be weary of life. At last, however, our army, not of its own, but prevailing by the power of Almighty God, drove the soldiers of the king of Bohemia into a neighboring river, where almost all of them were either slain by the sword, or suffocated by the river, or taken captive, and failed by the enemy. Thus, the flight of the guard availed itself of a few, for nearly all remained with us [either] captured, or dead. And although the aforesaid king saw the ranks of his soldiers scattered, and deserted almost by all, yet he still refused to yield to our victorious standards, but defended himself with a marvelous courage in manner and spirit, until some of our soldiers fell upon him, mortally wounded, together with his right-hand man. Then at length that great king lost his life in victory, whom not the strength of our power, but the right hand of the most high God, mercifully judging our cause, slew. We, therefore, humbly recognizing these and other benefits from him who brought them to us and referring to the praise and glory of his most holy name, to all that we knew to be acceptable to the most high king of God, the son of Jesus Christ, we will turn our concern with more devout readiness.

LETTER XXXIV. *Rudolph the victor indulges Ottocari's defeated children. (An. Dom. 1278, cod. Rud. xxxiv.)*

ARGUMENT.--Part of the diploma in which Rudolph shows his clemency, following the example of the best princes, towards the children of the children of the King of Bohemia, and bestows upon them his grace and love.

Rudolph, etc. [Augustus, king of the Romans always by the grace of God], to all forever. The divine princes, who directed the earthly empire both by arms and by laws, by the divine nod, attracted to themselves that power, as if properly their own, so that they thought no less to spare the vanquished and to pity the prostrate than to conquer the rebels and repress the proud. As the victorious power of the republic was moderated by mercy, so also, they made themselves endearing to their enemies and to their devotees. Desiring to follow in the footsteps of these princes and our elders, turning the eyes of our meekness with a merciful glance to the pupils of the erstwhile Ottocar [Ottogar], the illustrious king of Bohemia, we open the bosom of our grace and a safe refuge full of favor to the children themselves, etc.

LETTER XXXV. *Privilege of the city of Bruns in Moravia. (An. Dom. 1279, cod. Rud. 35.)*

ARGUMENT.--The liberties, customs, rights, and privileges approved by Ottokar to the Brunus state of Moravia, have been ratified, and some of them have been enlarged. It strengthens the immunity of things and persons by perpetual sanction. He decrees that the Jews should be subject to the burdens of citizens according to custom.

Desiring to expand the power of the Roman empire by mercy rather than by tyranny, we liberally open the veins of clemency to those who come to our port of refuge to ask for grace. Hence it is that we, our beloved and faithful citizens of Brunes, who have humbly submitted themselves and the city itself to our authority, to the fullness of our favor and grace, by our gracious will, confirm to the same citizens all and every liberties, rights , the privileges and customs which, or which they held from the dismissal of Ottocar, the illustrious king of Bohemia, without any contradiction. From which we extend some thanks to those present. In the first place, we want that the tax which the said king has deputed for the use of the same city for eight consecutive years, as it is said, should be collected for the use of the city for twelve consecutive years, adding four years to the grace of the said king. We decree this also, that the aforesaid citizens passing through different states and places of government for their needs, under the pretext of damages or promises made by the King of Bohemia to any person, should not be pledged in the means or persons. We also wish to continue with perpetual strength that favor which has hitherto passed through the lands of Bohemia and Moravia without payment of taxes. Furthermore, if the aforesaid citizens have proved with legitimate documents that the two towns of Curin and Streletz have been pledged to them by the king of Bohemia for three hundred and fifty marks, we attach one hundred and fifty marks to the same obligation, and thus they will be held as a pledge for five hundred marks. Moreover, the areas which formerly belonged to the use of the city should return to the benefit of the same city without prejudice to others. To these things we decreed with perpetual sanction, that no baron or nobleman of the land should presume to perpetrate any violence on the property or persons of the citizens within the walls of the city. Indeed, it is our heart that whatever immunity or liberty has been granted to these citizens by the generosity of the kings of Bohemia, and is still preserved intact, should continue to be constantly strengthened by law, and that no one should be afraid of any rash venture to injure our summit. We also judge the Jews in such a way that they do not violate the customs hitherto observed in supporting the burdens of the state together with the citizens.

LETTER XXXVI. *Rudolph informs the king of Hungary about the state of Bohemia and Moravia. (An. Dom. 1279, cod. Rud. 36.)*

ARGUMENT.--To Ladislaus, king of Hungary, whose merits he extols with praise for his strong assistance in the last conflict with Ottokar, he affirms with every assurance that neither treaty nor friendship will fail as long as he lives. that the bishop of Olomouc and the nobles of Moravia had done homage to him and to the government in the presence of the religious, who would also instruct him about the state of Bohemia. Hence his hostages were to be restored to him by the exchange of the existing Bohemian nobles with the Hungarians. He said that he would not accept John and his brothers, who had once offended both of them, into his favor and patronage, nor would he do so in the future, unless he himself, taking pity on them, had pardoned them.

To the great prince, etc. Rudolph, etc. The works of probity which your royal highness contributed to us at the time when it was necessary for us to experience the full constancy of your firm association and the infallible truth of your unblemished faith are luminous, and not only so that we may easily distinguish from others [Fors. Let the assurance be proved with us by the works of faith. The strong fortitude of your youthful mind has also merited, so that while we confer with us widely about our supporters and friends, we love you above all others. And although our beloved N. was once the husband of our daughter's illustrious daughter, as it is said, alas! The goal of a short life has passed too quickly, but the foundation of our association and friendship with you will remain immovable as long as we live. Of which, dearest son and friend, may you be certain and indubitable. Of course, religious men, certainly men who are fervently zealous for your honor, will clearly inform you of our progress in the kingdom of Bohemia, in whose presence I will come. The bishop of Olomouc, and certain barons of Moravia paid homage to us and to the Roman Empire. And although it would have been easy for us to subject both the kingdom and the children to extreme desolation, yet it seemed to many more healthful and more pleasing to God, that we should come to the attainment of your purpose and ours, without the perpetual extermination of so many people, and especially of the children. And let not your royal highness doubt that, whether the said assignment of the children to you is successful or not, we will continue your business in this part with faithful constancy as our own; and since some noble Bohemians are detained by your barons, through whom the restitution of your property might be easily promoted, we consult your serenity and beseech you from the bottom of our hearts, that you deign to labor for the liberation of four persons; the absolution of which, as we have said to your will and ours, [...] Moreover, Count John urges us much, that, having put aside from our hearts the injury done to us, we may gather him under the grace of protection who is willing to divert us: to whom we did not care to answer anything but that of the king and the kingdom We condescend to gather the devoted of Hungary to our services. And if by any chance your royal deference to the excesses of the said John and his brothers should lead them to pity, we earnestly request that mention be made of the innumerable damage inflicted on us by them in a hostile manner. We also assure you that we will in no way collect them without your express good pleasure, but if you take care to think about the revenge of a common injury, you will feel the benefit of our faithful and powerful help in these and all other matters.

LETTER XXXVII. *Rudolph writes to the supreme Roman Pontiff, and grants most liberally whatever the Roman Church has hitherto demanded of him. (An. Dom. 1277, cod. Rud. 37.)*

ARGUMENT.--Nicolas III, not long after his consecration, in his letter, repeated by his predecessors through the Messengers and the apostolic letters, renewing them in detail, reposes that he will obey his filial obedience as much as possible. He submits himself and the authority of the Holy See. He prays that he will kindly hear and direct his ambassadors concerning the coronation, the alliance with Charles, king of Sicily, and other affairs. And finally, the clergy, whom he had recently experienced as very generous, and all their causes, commends him again and again with great vehemence.

Most holy, etc. Rudolph, etc. The integrity of sincere devotion and the affections of the appropriate readiness, which coalesced around the sacrosanct Roman Church, our most pious mother, firmly rooted in our bosom long ago, but now in these last days, in which the providence of the supreme father of the apostolic father has provided for us and the Christian people for the vow, thus sprouts and grows more richly. He thus turned the interior of our mind into every path of justice, so that not only the suspicion of evil in us, by which the same mother Church might have made us notable, is now completely abolished, but also every appearance of evil, which could have been assessed by eye-witted conjecture, as a filial intention. which has never really turned astray, let it shine brighter and brighter, be completely cut off in the eyes of the father. Behold, therefore, all and everything that the alma mater Church has hitherto demanded from us, both by news and by special letters, liberally approving with benevolent applause and gratuitous assent, in these and all other things we conceive to conform equally to the apostolic favors, humbly supplicating to your most gracious holiness, in so far as we, and to direct the government entrusted to us by heaven for the honor of the Most High and the salvation of the Christian people by a providential dispensation, and also to support us with the benefit of apostolic grace. Furthermore, we most faithfully appoint the industrious and prudent men N. and N. at the feet of your beatitude, as the chief business, upon the friendship between us and the illustrious N. according to the counsel of your providence, if this should be settled by our wish, to consolidate, and above all other affairs of the Christian republic , which desire to be promoted by the energy of your piety, are guided by your nods and fuel. Therefore, we ask that our petitions, and especially those of our clerics, who present themselves to us with gratuitous and fruitful services and are very pleased and accepted, or who happen to present the same to your holiness through the ministry of their messengers, we beg to be effectively heard by the sweetness of your desired propitiation.

THE THIRD BOOK THE FIRST

LETTER I. *The electors of the Holy Roman Empire confirm the donation made by the emperor Rudolph to the first wife of the empress Anna. (An. Dom. 1279, cod. Rud. I.)*

ARGUMENT.--Holy Rom. imp. The electors approve the donation of a thousand marks of annual revenue made by Rudolph, king of the Romans, to his queen wife Anna, deputing them from the camp, lands, and possessions at her discretion, provided that their guardians promise by oath that, upon the queen's compliance with them, the revenue will be restored to the right of the empire.

The exceeding whiteness of the virtues and the praiseworthy presence of goodness, with which our illustrious lady Queen Anne is predicably adorned, gratify us by refreshing us from the delight of her fragrance in such a way, and delight in gratifying us, that we willingly rise to increase her honor and advantage, and to everything that may advance her salvation. We are liberally invited. This is why we want to know you all, that we agree together with our other collectors in this voluntary movement, and we give full and free consent, that our most serene lord Rudolph, the honorable companion of his person, the same our lady in goods, camps, lands, and other possessions up to a thousand marks of gold, paid in places more convenient for him, and where he sees more expedient, he may be able to assign, to be peacefully possessed by our lady herself for the time of her life; so, however, that the guardians of camps, lands, and possessions of this kind, bind themselves by this oath, that as soon as our lady Anne, the illustrious queen, is removed from the midst, they will faithfully restore and restore the same goods to the property and right of the empire.

LETTERS

LETTER II. *A certain city congratulates Rudolph on his successful achievements. (An. Dom. 1277, cod. Rud. II.)*

ARGUMENT.--When the report reached the remote provinces of the empire that Rudolph had reduced Austria and the other provinces to his power, a certain city of faithful subjects congratulated the king on the successful outcome, and, promising a more successful one, begged him not to condescend to express the truth of the matter by letters written to him.

Most excellent, etc. No. A state of the promptest obedience of devout fidelity. We give as much thanks as we can to Almighty God, that he has chosen to give justice to the royal cause, as we have heard, so that everything may succeed with the plans and actions of your serenity. Of which the credulity of our devotion and faith, easily applied to that which he desires, blossoms in joy with the joys of conception, ardently desiring the fruit of the knowledge of the most certain truth. Wherefore we beseech your majesty with the most reverential devotion, in so far as concerning your proceedings and successes, which may the justice of divine providence, by promoting them well, guard and lead to better things, that you would be willing to declare the avid faith of our devotion to the truth of the royal writings, so that the joy which the prone credulity of the devout conceived in the hearing, into the harbor may the infallible truth of your majesty bring about the desired certainty, whose power it is to command and forbid, and to decree as it pleases, to whom it is convenient.

LETTER III. *The same with the above letter of argument. (An. Dom. 1279, cod. Rud. III.)*

ARGUMENT.--Another city hearing of the notable victory of the king of the Bohemians in daring to rebel against Rudolph the most just prince, signifies to him that he exults with joy at his recent triumph, and begs him with the utmost devotion, that he may deign to send them royal letters, anxious for the most certain news of his great glory.

Most serenely, etc. No. The city prepared itself for all obedience. Of necessity, the promise of divine truth must be unshakable, and all power is crushed to nothingness, which is shared against the command of the supreme prince. For it is written that nothing evil can be done against a righteous king when he sits on the throne, and it is the Spirit of God who speaks, against whom all arrogance is gathered together in vain to lift itself up. We have heard, most just king, that some have assumed the audacity of rebellion against the royal majesty, and that they have attempted to oppose the seat of justice; whom your excellency triumphantly overcame, subdued to a level the rough barriers, caused the hardness to soften, and the enemy's elevations to have no stable horns. Upon which our hearts are filled with the joys of conception, and do not cease to bloom again in royal happiness, with the fresh ornaments of dances. For this is the chief ardor of our mind, these inmost wishes, that your sublimity may be gathered to all the fences of prosperity by constant growth. True, because the more effectually declared are more effective, and the more joyfully the glorious assertion of the prince enters, we most devoutly beseech the sacred royal majesty, inasmuch as you wish to speed up something about the processes which divine providence supplies, by which our devotion, eager for your exaltations, may be most safely fostered among those adepts of the methods of happy tranquility.

LETTERS

LETTER IV. *He undertakes a certain defense of the devastated monastery. (An. Dom. 1279, cod. Rud. IV.)*

ARGUMENT.--Rudolphus, on the motion of the abbot N., who complained that many injuries had been inflicted on his monastery by perverse men, that monastery, the brothers, things, and persons pertaining to the same, commits N. to the abbot's desire, commanding him by royal authority, so that no one thereafter He allows himself to be subject to trouble.

With the diadem of imperial dignity and the right hand of strength holding the scepter insignia, while we search the secretary of our mind, turning, what anointing, what the scepter, what the royal crown signifies, given to us divinely, in the sacred oil of libation, with which the royal arms are anointed, clemency or mercy to the afflicted and we clearly understand, gather and weigh the exercise of the oppressed, the preeminence in the crown, the power to defend the oppressed in the scepter by the right hand of courage. For this reason, it is our heart to protect all subjects of the Roman Empire, especially churches and ecclesiastical persons from the attacks of any evildoers, and to be able to rise with all our might to repress the cunning of the perverts. Indeed, the honorable man N., abbot of the monastery of N., came to our presence, lamentably complaining to us that some, seduced by the impulses of evil spirits, not fearing God, nor respecting men, had done many injuries to his monastery in its people and possessions by robbery and plunder. Fearing therefore the same venerable father and conjecturing the worst of the events of the past, he humbly besought our majesty, that we might commit the aforesaid monastery to your devotion, with all its possessions, to be defended against the attacks of evil men. We, therefore, bowed down to his prayers, have led the present to require the purity of your faith, nevertheless commanding and granting you by royal authority, in so far as you maintain, protect, and defend on our behalf the aforesaid monastery and the assembly of the brothers, the people, their possessions, movable and immovable goods, and not only everything belonging to the monastery itself, and do not allow yourself to be unduly molested by anyone from now on and in the past.

LETTER V. *Rudolph to the king of France congratulating him on the contract with him (An. Dom. 1279, cod. Rud. V.)*

ARGUMENT.--When, through the marriage of his daughter Clementia, won by Nicholas III, to Charles Martell, the nephew of Charles, king of Sicily, he had contracted the desired affinity with the illustrious house of France, he joyfully conveyed the matter to King Philip III in the most dutiful letters, promising that his benevolence would be opportunely useful.

Among all the rest of the insignia of Augustan titles bestowed upon us by God, among the many auspicious wishes of happiness, with which the right hand of the Lord has encircled our sides, it has incessantly smiled upon our hearts with a truly sweet kiss, and fertilized our heart with the cup of immense joy, which is between us and you, in which indeed the vigor of the forefathers spread strength and courage, friendly marriages of kinship were contracted. These things are the more inseparable, the more inseparable we intend not only to keep always, but also to strengthen, by which it pleases us the more desirable to be united with the illustrious house of France. We therefore beg of us that your royal highness will receive the proofs of our letters with fuller confidence, that our solicitude will not be lacking in opportunities for you, but that he will dutifully show himself benevolent and vindictive to all that we know to increase your honor and glory.

LETTERS

LETTER VI. *Rudolph writes to the state praising his certain fidelity. (An. Dom. 1279, cod. Rud. VI.)*

ARGUMENT.--To the citizens of Tuscany, who had testified their loyalty to the Roman empire, he replied that he would highly recommend it to the Roman Pontiff, and sent an ambassador to it, who proposed some things to be put into execution in his name.

Rudolph, etc. We received with kind affection your letters which you addressed to the summit of the kingdom, expressive of your devotion and of the faith which you bear to the sacred government. Of course, we follow the memorable constancy of your honesty, which decorated you in the affairs of the government, for his commendation regarding those things which regard your quiet and your advanced stages, intending to concentrate vigilantly, with our most holy father, the lord supreme pontiff, so that he may claim for you a shelter of paternal benevolence, our cares and works. as much as we can afford. Moreover, we exhort the prudence of your university more attentively, and we ask that, in so far as the beloved N. family over what he has proposed to you in our name, you will not hesitate to apply faith and to impart the beneficence of the appropriate results, so that for this reason we may always be specially bound to you in all that we know will be beneficial to you.

LETTER VII. *Rudolph regrets that some of his land has passed unrecognized. (An. Dom. 1279, cod. Rud. VII.)*

ARGUMENT.--The prince's best friend was pleasantly pleased, that, while running through the provinces of Austria, both of them had exchanged the consolation of conversation. An ambassador sends an interpreter of mutual apology.

Rudolph, etc. The fact that your passage through the districts of our country was so clandestine and hasty, that we were not permitted to recuperate the comfort of your lovely vision and address, has generated for us not a slight matter of internal disturbance, so that you can calmly delight us with one heart and one soul. In fact, we grieve more intensely over it, which we trust has affected you even more, instead of enjoying our more important presence. So that the remedial benefit of a friendly apology may interpose here and there over these, see that No. credential, etc.

LETTER VIII. *Rudolph forms a kind of friendship with the cardinal. (An. Dom. 1279, cod. Rud. VIII.)*

ARGUMENT.--SRE the cardinal, whose name was celebrated on the lips of all in Germany, as being very powerful in counsel and authority at the holy see, and with whom he had a rare exchange of letters, so that he may have more frequently in the future, he wishes to add to his relationship, and he hopes to follow him and speak before him shortly .

Venerable, etc. Rudolph, etc. So many and so many reports of your virtuous deeds among us have been invalidated, so many and so many reports of your alma mater Church of laudable fame, your ministerial plan is decorated with insignia and is adorned with titles of exceptional authority, which greatly pleases us to enter into an alternate familiarity with you, comfort and mutual affection conforming to the sweetness [... Therefore, although we have hitherto been distant from you due to the incapacity of places, the rare letter of our greeting has suggested the interior of our minds, although we have not been refreshed by the frequent address of your letters, yet the stream of hope conceived from your benevolence does not cease to flow, but is constantly enriched by growth. For hereafter, seizing the opportunity, we intend not only to visit you by letter, but in the near future, as the Most High Guide, to present ourselves to you in person, so that the affection of our grateful love may grow by successive concrete steps into profuse and profitable palms of gracious shoots. Behold then the honorable, etc.

LETTER IX. *Rudolph writes to the cardinal recommending himself and the affairs of the government. (An. Dom. 1279, cod. Rud. IX.)*

ARGUMENT.--The orator, or his procurator at the holy see, is much praised by all the ambassadors returning to Rome, he entices him with the hope of rewards, and he adds to the indulgence of the king's favor and benevolence the zeal of the king, so that he may proceed laudably to his business and that of the empire.

Rudolph, etc. To the honorable and prudent man N., etc. The increasing and faithful report of our tidings returning from the Roman court at different times, of the praises of your most pure faith, which you unweariedly bear to us and the empire, has been woven and spread in such profuse publicity throughout the county, that we are diligently engrossed in the submission of your gracious devotion, and we are fervently attracted to them. , which we know of the increase of your honor as well as of your approach. We have, therefore, with the utmost affection, exhorted your honesty, in so far as you are assured of the gracious privilege of our benevolence, that you will not cease to pursue the cares and labors of your laudable purpose concerning us and our affairs with the duty of a more laudable continuation.

LETTERS

LETTER X. *The citizens of Leodia complain of certain clerics. (An. Dom. 1279, cod. Rud. X.)*

ARGUMENT.--The citizens of Leodien were disturbed by a privilege granted to the clergy of the city in ancient times, and renewed and declared by Rudolph, which had recently been published by the same: for by this the laws of the city and of the whole province, founded by the predecessors of the same Rudolph, were subverted; they take refuge in him with complaints of circumvention, so that since the founder of the law is himself the interpreter and chastiser of the same, he may conciliate the peace of the state and the province by abrogating that privilege.

To his most serene master, the citizens of Leodien, etc. Because by the ordinance of God, from whom all power proceeds, the supreme power of your republic is acknowledged to be attributed to clemency, so that by the vigor of your greatness justice may be preserved, and injuries may be rooted out, the weakness of the faithful may be relieved, and the rebellion of the strong may be suppressed, directing all things by the just balance of the laws in the service of the Savior, to the majesty recalling your clemency from the penultimate ends of the Roman empire, under the confidence of your grace we have brought to the special royal highness, not without sorrow and perturbation of heart, to intimate that the honorable men and clergy of the city N., although we worship him with all the reverence we can, yet the city and the whole of our country rest in peace and peace impatience, when we suspected nothing of them against the enemy, a certain privilege hitherto unheard of by your majesty, as they claim, has been renewed, confirmed, or even declared recently among us, in the presence of many. That which was perceived and brought into publication, although it disturbed the whole multitude as if by sudden thunder-strokes and terror of lightning, yet because of your veneration of the blessed name we heard it reverently, and the abundance of it received, and with a mature deliberation upon it prevented, because by the same, if it should be called a privilege, the whole the law of the state and of our country are almost entirely absorbed, and the general state of our country, ordered from ancient times by your pious predecessors, is discolored; to amend, of which it is to be composed, to the audience of your majesty, which we believe to be surrounded in this part by the artifice of obtaining, under a certain form we have decided to proclaim it in common and solemnly. Hoping, and trusting in the Most High, that with you the obvious inconveniences and dangers arising from such a privilege, your provident and benevolent wisdom, watching over the remedies of the faithful subjects, will relieve us from so many disturbances and the grievances of the whole country, and to a peaceful and ancient state, cut off from noxious novelties, He will reform everything wholesomely.

LETTER XI. *Rudolph exhorts the citizens of Maguntine to harmony. (An. Dom. 1280, cod. Rud. XI.)*

ARGUMENT.--Admonished by the legate of Mainz of the simultaneity between the citizens and the ministers, who had decided to take the matter to arms: and at the same time being asked to meet the imminent conflagration of the royal objects by authority, he replied that prudence and restraint should be used, that the narrow swords might be put down by the rivals. For the same purpose he had deputed Count G. to put out the conflagration by communicating plans with him.

Rudolphus, etc., to the citizens of Maguntine. The odious disturbance of the rising discord, which is taking place in your borders at the same time, has lately been exposed by the industrious man of the royal highness N., stings us with the sting of compassion so much the harder, inasmuch as we feel that the troubles of the whole earth are brought down from it, willing our efforts willingly and liberally to extinguish the conflagration itself. to apply Of course it seemed to us expedient, and we advise in good faith that, preventing the expenses of such a ruin, you who are keen-eyed animals should tread the path of modesty in this article of the case. Let us swear that, when you enter into the ministry, you will direct that line of rectitude, which the form of the oath presupposes upon the common peace, that no injury shall be touched at all, but that you will fervently endeavor to bring the same ministers to the union of peace and concord. For thus saving you and your houses, the neighboring fire may be applied to the walls. Because a house built in the midst of a conflagration, even if it is not consumed by the fire, is nevertheless weakened, the strength of the framework being exhausted to the point of collapse. Therefore, we beseech and exhort more attentively, inasmuch as, as soon as you leap into the midst of the extermination, endeavor to repair the differences of so great a division by the control of innate prudence. And behold, within three days after the withdrawal of your news of our presence, we propose to depute the noble man Count G. to your presence for this reason, so that by his cooperative counsel the tight swords may be snatched from the hands of the contenders by you.

LETTER XII. *Rudolph writes of the same agreement to the clergy of Mainz. (An. Dom. 1280, cod. Rud. XII.)*

ARGUMENT.--The clergy of Moguntine, having been urged by the prayers of the foreseeer of the future losses, puts in the same cause, that if he pleases, he will make effective efforts by setting fire to it, so that the outcome will soon be made public.

Rudolphus, etc., dean and chapter of Mainz. The cruel straits of tribulations and calamities, with which a warlike attack threatens to invade your borders, we must have sympathized with a more compassionate feeling, as we feel that from these more pernicious crises spring. Because of this, stimulated by your fervent allurements to the stable good of concord, and to rooting out completely the seeds of simultaneity, we willingly intend to interpose our parts effectively and diligently, as the author of the Lord, the evidence of the work will teach you.

LETTER XIII. *Rudolph provides a certain order to the house of the Penitents. (An. Dom. 1280, cod. Rud. XIII.)*

ARGUMENT.--Grieving that the religious house of penitent women is very badly managed in spiritual and temporal matters, SRE strongly prays to the cardinal to obtain the removal of the providers from the supreme pontiff, and to entrust it to the provincial house of the Friars Minor with the ability to enter the cloister for administering the sacraments of the Church.

Because in our city N. there is a certain regular house of the order of the Penitents, which is said to suffer a lack both in spiritual and temporal provisions, we ourselves sympathize with that house more urgently, as the weakness of that sex is nearer to the case, we implore your fatherhood with the greatest affection we can, and we exhort, inasmuch as the persons of the aforesaid house from their servants, who now preside over them [there], carelessness, might incur serious harm to their reputation and their health, to procure with our most beloved father, the lord supreme pontiff, the effect that they should be disgraced, that the house itself from the servants of such useless bonds absolute, of the rest of the provincial provision of the Friars Minor, that the change of the Exalted be made about the same right hand. So that the persons themselves in the former order of permanent Penitents, the aforesaid provincial in his own right, or suitable brethren of his order, may exercise the office of visitation and correction over them, and the brethren themselves may be permitted to provide for this purpose by deputing the Penitents themselves to enter the cloister to administer the ecclesiastical sacraments, when appropriate.

LETTER XIV. *Someone from the Roman court recommended a certain Rudolph to the emperor. (An. Dom. 1280, cod. Rud. XIV.)*

ARGUMENT.--The procurator of the king of the Romans in the city commends N. to him in the best way his merit in the matter of coronation, so that by the reward and honors of the same affection he may be an example to others, which they will follow with zeal of mind.

Most serenely, etc. It is recognized that it belongs to the increase of your glory, if those who have been commended to your highness should receive the rewards of their honesty, by which example the others may be inspired from good to better. Wherefore, since the discreet man N. stood by us faithfully in the business of your exaltation, and showed himself to be commendable, promoting your honor by his own strength, I commend him as much as possible to your excellency, earnestly imploring your majesty for the same, so much so that when he came to you, he would receive royal clemency. to receive kindly, and in all respects to treat him graciously, liberally imputing to him the effect of both due justice and your grace, so that both he and the others, challenged by a similar example, may endeavor to hasten to the service of your greatness.

LETTERS

LETTER XV. *A certain bishop explains to Rudolph the grievances of his episcopate. (An. Dom. 1280, cod. Rud. XV.)*

ARGUMENT.--The bishop, being affected by many favors from Rudolph, and so much bound to him, bore it with great difficulty that he could not follow him to the solemnity of the coronation, because his see was heavy with foreign air and exposed to the intrigues of his neighbors; He excuses himself, promising that he will not be lacking in obedience after his return.

Greetings to the most serene lord N. bishop with obedience, all reverence and honor. From the abundance of the royal generosity I confess that I have liberally received more than many thanks and concessions, which have convinced me of such self-efficacy, that although I am bound by the duty of subjection to the fidelity of the royal majesty, yet in this respect the enlarged will exceeds the debt, and in the same respect the debt itself, although in be it great, it is almost of no importance. Wherefore I offer myself, and mine, and all that I am, entirely to your excellency; not despairing of finding favor with God, with whom, in the abyss of bestowals and graces, he placed the most suitable seat for himself. I therefore humbly request that, patiently attending to the royal serenity which is here designated as the office of the style, he may excuse me from these, spare me, and bear me, preserving his favor to me nevertheless. Of course, when I personally arrived anew at the episcopate entrusted to me, in my new arrival I entered a new labyrinth of debtors, I was so oppressed on every side by the fury of the creditors, I was harassed with importunity, that there was scarcely enough time for counsels, scarcely enough income, with which I would be able to check the mouths of the intruders, with which I could stop the pestilential cries to check the credits. And to add to these misfortunes, the noble neighbors of my episcopate violently seize the rights of competition, they not only obstruct my jurisdiction, but, as far as it is in them, they utterly endeavor to weaken it. They could daily cause much trouble to me and to the Roman Empire, if there were no one to resist their efforts. To whom also he gives in my helper of harm, which, etc. Because of these and other things, I am so exhausted with money, so stripped of my resources, that at present I am immovable to pursue the promised reddar, bound by other insolubles, my physical infirmity, which may be odious to me, yet becomes an indefatigable companion, adding to these importunities a pile of scrupulous disturbance and trouble. Because of which the royal majesty, taking pity on me in these things, takes me out of the way for his coronation, mercifully relieves me, and learns to pity my impotence. For on his happy return, when he returns with the assumed triumphal crown, I will visit you in person, and at the grateful expense of the service, I will certainly not fail to redeem the slowness of the past.

LETTER XVI. *He commends the newly elected bishop to the counts and barons, etc. (An Dom. 1275, cod. Rud. XVI.)*

ARGUMENT.--Siffridus, the archbishop of Colonia, who was sent to him by Gregory X at Lyons, and recommended to him, that he should not allow the most turbulent of the time to the church and the diocese, and those insulting his archbishops, not to pass without royal protection, he recommended to the counts and the rest in such a way that they would know that they would do him harm as well , and to offend the royal majesty: they render the obedience of fidelity both to themselves and to him, and, having forgotten their former entanglements, they worship a peaceful peace henceforth.

Rudolphus, etc., to all the counts, barons, etc. The God of infinite mercy, having for a long time already afflicted the city and the diocese, H. watching with the eyes of compassion and mercy, excluded and removed from the dangers of wars and other adversities, knowing about the shepherd, willing and able to relieve the aforementioned city and diocese, depressed until now not without the faults of men, as we believe, and he deigned to provide mercifully for the honorable man N. Indeed, this man, who is very well known to our most holy father, and the more he is known, the more favored he is, has brought back to us the benefits of many commendations. Further, we are instructed by the admonitions and commands of our most holy father, the said N. and his church with all those entrusted to him, both by virtue of his honesty, and by the most gracious intervention of our beloved father, desiring to pursue with a special feeling of grace and favor, all the injuries, if now it should happen to support, to ascribe to us those who are willing, and those who are worthy to pursue them as our own, therefore we command you, under the protection of our grace, firmly and strictly, inasmuch as the same N. elected to our dearest prince, a member of the Holy Roman Empire, as your bishop, intending in all things faithfully and devoutly, so that the obedience of your fidelity deserves merit both with our majesty and with his paternal providence. And you, with your father himself, in the pleasantness of peace and tranquility of mind, able to rest with the new growing material of joys after wiping away your tears.

LETTER XVII. *Privilege of the city Hall. (An. Dom. 1280, cod. Rud. XVII.)*

ARGUMENT.--Rudolphus Hallens gives the city of Suevia, due to the constant obedience rendered to him and the government, a royal bountiful liberty, so that citizens of both sexes cannot pursue their causes, or be called to judgment outside the city of Hallens.

To this we know that we have been called to the summit of the highest dignity by the supreme and first founder of all kingdoms, that with all those placed under the protection of our government we must exist easily in law, or in the exhibition of law, and liberal in grace, we lead them to impart greater grace and the fullness of greater grace worthy of, who are carried away by no storms of adversity from our services and those of the government. Since, therefore, the beloved sons of the city of Halle have expended and are expending such devoted services of fidelity to us, that their prayers may deserve the grace of hearing from our majesty and the effect they desire, we are inclined to their humble prayers, and as a special grace we surrender to them this liberty, which has been handed down , and we confirm the granting of the royal authority by the protection of the present decree, that no citizen of the city of Halles of either sex shall be called upon to stand trial outside the city of Halles, whether real or personal, or if any other action is attempted against him. Nay, if anyone has any action against any of the aforesaid citizens, he shall prosecute it before the judge of the city in the same order of law, etc. None, then, etc.

LETTER XVIII. *Rudolph commends the Cologne elect to the Roman Pontiff. (An. Dom. 1275, cod. Rud. XVIII.)*

ARGUMENT.--Siffridus, the canonically elected archbishop of Colonia, who resides with the pontiff of Lyons, speaks with many praises, and prays that he may send him as soon as possible, consecrated and adorned with the sacred mantle, to his seat exposed to great calamities, unless perhaps he decides to exalt him to a more exalted place.

Among the rest, whose vigilance worries us, whose desirable campaign unceasingly stirs our minds, we believe that it is really expedient for the peaceful state of the holy mother Church, the reformation of the separation of the empire, and the relief of the Holy Land, that the churches of the kingdom of Germany, destitute of pastors, may flourish again by the substitution of new sponsors, and provision the desired comfort will be recreated. Among whom, indeed, the more eminently venerable the church of Cologne resists, the more it is attacked by the storms of severe persecutions, and driven by the calamities of monstrous disturbances, the more quickly it needs to be relieved by the aid of your paternal provision. And because N., according to the laudable testimony of many, from the beginning of his youth he was always a group packed with virtues, and distinguished by the preaching of honorable conduct and life; for that we beseech your beatitude most piously, with the greater affection that we can, inasmuch as the church itself will knowingly demand to be governed by its salutary government, and to be comforted by its lovely presence, that you deign as much as possible to destine the same chosen one to govern the church itself, speedily expedient by the compassion of innate paternal clemency, unless perhaps he himself of a more sublime place to the government, for which he is without a doubt deemed fit, your pious consideration, having obtained his manifold probity, has decided to depute him. Indeed, it is most certainly hoped that through him, as if by an immovable pillar, the government will be supported, and in the house of the Lord the same elect will nevertheless sprout like a fruitful olive tree.

LETTER XIX. *Rudolph commends to Philip the king of the Franks the monastery of the Golden Valley of the Cistercian order. (An. Dom. 1276, cod. Rud. XIX.)*

ARGUMENT.--Rudolphus, being asked by the Cistercians of the cloister of the Golden Valley of the Diocese of Trier, to place them under the patronage of the King of France, since they were placed in the extreme ends of the empire and were suffering serious troubles from unrighteous men, he explained to the same king the petitions of the monks, and fully complied with their wishes.

In the lofty thrones of kings, and in any other tribunals of power, which the light of the Catholic faith illumines, where they are especially contiguous by the ability of places, that conformity of vows must especially prevail, that indissociability of minds must be strengthened, so that they may be recreated by the imminent expense of one another, by the effective consolation of alternate compassion. Which of course, because we gladly offer you for your serenity, and that will benefit you [in] your opportunities, we offer the same from you under the confidence of firm hope not undeservedly in return. Of course, it contained a petition extended to us by the religious men of N. and N. abbots, and the assembly of the Golden Valley of the Cirsterian order, that with them, being very separated from the heart of the Roman empire, and established at the extreme ends of the same empire under the umbrella of imperial protection, it would not be permitted for them to breathe fiercely, with you we would deign to assist them, because you would have intended their rest and peace with effect [affection]. Because, therefore, we trust in your royal kindness that [in] the heaven given to your hearts by the propagation of the ardor of sincere devotion by your illustrious progenitors, you apply your cares and labors to our desires on this pious business; We have diligently exhorted your highness, as far as divine piety, reverence for the orders, and for your safety, the aforesaid abbot and congregation, according to the restraint of the privilege granted to them, in all possessions, men and persons, rights and things of all kinds, by whatever name they may be considered, and wherever they are in the government, and not only over all the liberties granted to them by whomsoever, against whomsoever the aforesaid government, of whatever condition they may exist, who violently or injuriously extort against them the aid, patronage, and relief of your gracious defense and timely protection, from the king's kindness, so disdain willingly and liberally to be continually imparted. For this will doubtless yield you to the accumulation of merit with God, and to the growth of a magnificent name among men, if you maintain the said monastery and persons in their right, the same insulters, evildoers, as if your subjects were worthy of punishment.

LETTER XX. *Rudolph revokes and makes void all the privileges granted and to be granted contrary to the previous letter. (An. Dom. 1277, cod. Rud. XX)*

ARGUMENT.--When certain privileges of theft and robbery were shown to be contrary to the aforesaid subjection, Rudolph declares that both those previously granted and those subsequently granted, which conflict with the same, are void and of no force.

Because we remember that we have called upon the illustrious and magnificent prince Lord Philip, King of the Franks, by special letters, protected by our royal authority, to offer and afford to the religious men of the abbot and convent of the monastery of the Golden Valley of the Cistercian order against any insolence of the invaders, a suitable protection and relief, and we ourselves, the abbot and convent, are greatly desirous to be perpetually shared in the defense of the same king, we brought it to be decided by those present, that whatever has already been obtained by us through the suggestion of falsehood and the suppression of truth by those who have already obtained our grace, or may happen to be obtained in the future, is entirely lacking in the strength of firmness, for we revoke it as null and void, etc.

LETTER XXI. *Rudolph sends an ambassador to make peace between the prince and the citizens. (An. Dom. 1279, cod. Rud. XXI.)*

ARGUMENT.--Rudolph, fearing that the discord of the prince N. with his citizens might produce more serious losses, sends him an ambassador to interpret the peace, to whom, as if he were to lend an easy ear to him: this means that no greater and more acceptable obedience could be rendered to him by him, that he might break his anger by the flattery of his words .

We are truly anxious about your quiet and peaceful state by frequent meditation, the more we are constantly anxious in our inner hearts about the stable good of concord between you and our citizens, the greater security is promised from its votive consolidation, and the more serious losses we foresee prepared by dissension. Of course, because, among other things, we may feel more desirable a salutary union of concord, adapted to our wishes, see that N., the fervent of your honor, undoubtedly zealous for your presence, for this reason as an imaginary of our presence, we most trustfully intend, most affectionately beseeching you, in so far as he acquiesces in his exhortations, which he proposes to you in our name for our respect and that of the government, nay, even by your own instinct of convenience, if you endeavor to incline or apply your mind effectively and finally to peace, it will be known most certainly that in no case, in no event at all, will you be able to present to us so acceptable and so peaceful a submission. For this reason, we ask you to apply the same full faith to all, as to ours.

LETTER XXII. *Rudolph recommends a certain canon of the Church of Leodien, and that they send him as soon as possible to the court. (An. Dom. 1279, cod. Rud. XXII.)*

ARGUMENT.--He pursues the church of Leodien with excellent praise, and shows that he is ready to protect and honor it. Then A., having recruited his courtier into his college of canons, whom he sends to meet in possession, begs to be sent back to him as much as possible, he will be more useful to the business of the church in the royal court than in the choir of Leodence.

That noble church, the insignificant mirror of the kingdom of Germany, which is continually placed in the eyes of our benevolent grace and gracious benevolence, thus gratifies our mind with its excellent brightness, thus illuminates the innermost minds of our minds with the light of its splendor, which, of course, in the fragrance of its sweetness, as in a field full of fragrance, whom the Lord has blessed, we rejoice most of all. Therefore, not undeservedly, there is a readiness in us, willingly to focus on our interests, and to aspire to increasing honors with all the readiness of the spirit. Of course it is permissible for the honorable man A., who, by his excellent and demanding merits, to rise in great favor in the eyes of the region, may, by our permission, come to your presence, for the service of his first residence in your church, with the devotion which he is apt to offer, because, however, the condition and state of the same church circumstances provide for the balance, and we think it more profitable for us and far more advisable for your church, that he should still serve the same of your church in our court than in the choir; We beseech your prudence with the affection which we are able to extend, inasmuch as over the same residence for our own respect and benefit, pursuing him with due grace, you will endeavor as much as possible to send him back to our court, for your and the church's foreordained services, and there he will establish more fruitful ones, knowing most assuredly that because of the stages of advantages, that which may come to you from thence, let us always be more prompt in your dealings than any of them.

LETTER XXIII. *Rudolph confirms the opinion of the bishop of Leodia about fixing the boundaries of the duels. (An. Dom. 1279, cod. Rud. XXIII.)*

ARGUMENT.--The decree of the bishop of Leodence concerning the extension of the day set aside for the particular contest, at the discretion of the prince of the empire before whom it is to be fought, is valid in the whole province of Leodence, and the royal authority commands that it be observed by all.

Rudolphus, etc., to eminent noblemen, ministers, vassals, and all men subject to the episcopate of Leodence. To the presidents of us lately in our city N. for the tribunal solemnly on the Sabbath, etc., and the procurator of the venerable bishop of Leodia, our dearest prince, appearing there, for the requisition and justice of the same person, the group of all those around applauding and also approving, it was decided by sentence, that any prince of the government having temporal jurisdiction, whatever the condition may be, before whom they are accustomed to engage in duels, if on the day appointed, or set for the combatants for the conflict, for reasons necessary and honorable, he is not able to take part in this duel in person, by a convenient and useful change of plan, without any injury of the parties, the same leader may tacitly fix the day for another for his convenience, and prolong the conflict of the duel until a more convenient time. It is for this reason that we, by royal authority, having solemnly approved the said sentence, having duly passed it, solemnly approving it, have decided to enjoin your university by an edict, in so far as upon the prolongation of the duels of this kind, which by the venerable A. the forementioned bishop has hitherto happened or will happen in the future, to be humbly and devoutly prepared for him. in which it is appropriate for those who intend

LETTER XXIV. *Rudolph again commends the monastery of the Golden Valley to the king of the Franks. (An. Dom. 1277, cod. Rud. XXIV.)*

ARGUMENT.--The Cistercian convent of the Golden Valley of Luxemburg again commends Philip III to the king of the Franks, according to the form of the former letters: for he had not yet heard that he had accepted their patronage.

Although the religious men, the abbots, and the congregations of the monastery of the Golden Valley must breathe under the umbrella of the imperial power, because they are generally acting at a distance from us, under the fierce tyranny of perverts, whose slanderous insults you will be able to easily restrain, we have taken to imploring your serenity more attentively, inasmuch as according to our patents the continence of the letters which we have previously directed to your royal highness for their protection, kindly and graciously deign to impart to them the benefit and comfort of your protection and protection, so that you may thereby obtain favor with God and men more abundantly, and that we may be more readily experienced in your actions if the occasion arises.

LETTER XXV. *Rudolph takes the Hospitallers of the Teutonic house under his special protection. (An. Dom. 1285, cod. Rud. XXV.)*

ARGUMENT.--The Knights Hospitallers, or the house of St. Mary the Teutonics from Rom. the pontiff, cultivated and greatly increased by the emperors in spiritual and temporal matters, following in their footsteps, receives under special protection, and confirms and renews all their privileges, liberties and immunities, affixing his seal to the diploma.

In many ways and in various ways, the Christian people, radiant with the command of different virtues, and the glorious, sacred and happy Roman empire, was preferred to all the principalities of the world, and he made it superior to all barbarian nations in the past, and he will make it Lord of all in the future. Of course, for the protection of the state, springing from the twin stock, and thereby fortifying his force, he confederated the militia and the earthly kingdom of Judah with the Levitical tribe, and with the help of both swords, the control of the priesthood, and in turn the royal authority consolidates and strengthens the dignity of the priesthood, so that the eminence of each of the two is emphasized. and the malice of the perverse is spread beyond the limits of the world. Because of this, not so much in our arms and armed soldiers, or in the leaders of wars, but in the devout intercessions of the religious who constantly serve God, and in other pious works, the anchor of our hope is fixed, and by the shining of our glory, it is raised more sublimely and solidly into the mirror of the throne. Therefore, it behooves those who lead a religious life to look forward to their own interests, and to ward off inconvenient situations, to prevent future dangers. And among the rest, those who deserve especially our favor and benevolence, who support the most pious hospitality and the defense of the republic, as well as other works of piety, who, having thrown away their possessions, abdicated of their own will, and disdained the torture of their bodies, coming up from the opposite side, for the Roman empire and for they are not afraid to expose themselves to the wall of the house of Israel, and to redden the mantles of their souls in their own blood for the Catholic faith and the laws of their fathers. Like the venerable and beloved master and brothers in Christ of the Hospitallers of St. Mary's Teutonic House in Jerusalem, whose holy religion, having earned special grace from the imperial favors, and obtained the indulgence of many liberties and privileges, the apostolic seat took its beginning in the spiritual, and the flowery garden of the imperial court, The plant and structure of the emperors had as much growth from no princes as from the emperors in temporal affairs, since they have no other advocate or defender besides the Roman king. Therefore, of the divine memory of N. the emperor, following in the footsteps of other predecessors, adhering to the said house both in the head and in the members, the brothers and confreres of the same house, and not only their subjects managing their affairs, with all the goods movable and immovable which they reasonably possess throughout the entire Roman empire at the present time , and by just title they shall be able to obtain in future, whether they be states, etc., we receive under our special protection, and we approve all the privileges, liberties, and immunities, and any writings, which have been justly and reasonably granted and revoked by the said emperors and kings and confirming the present we renew, by affixing the seal of our majesty to the printer, confirming the present page.

LETTER XXVI. *Rudolph receives the brothers of the Hospital of St. John in Jerusalem under protection and confirms their privileges. (An. Dom. 1285, cod. Rud. XXVI.)*

ARGUMENT.--The Knights of St. John of Jerusalem fighting fearlessly against the Saracens for the defense of the Christian religion and the Catholic faith, he is exhorted to receive under special protection together with all their goods both acquired and to be acquired, and confirms and restores all the privileges, donations, and rights which Frederick II and they had obtained it from their predecessors.

Even if the generosity of benevolence proceeds from royalty, the universal [universal] professors [professions] of regular respect [professions] should share the solicitous protection and patronage of grace, yet the honorable brothers of the holy order of the hospital of St. , and their military insignia reddened in the blood of glorious martyrdom, fighting vigorously with the barbarian nations and not afraid to surrender themselves to a precious death, they should be so much more attentively supported by the arm of the royal highness in everything, and so much more highly honored, the more fervently they are distinguished for the defense of the Catholic faith in the military camp of Dominic. He knew, etc. Because, therefore, the pre-eminent order of the brothers of the Hospital of St. John of Jerusalem, whose sanctity, indeed, smells like the smell of the full field, which the Lord has blessed, has heartily refreshed us with the pleasure of sweetness, we embrace the prerogatives of singular favor, and because the order is recognized by titles evident from the ancient flourishing, and by excellent endowments of honors and liberties to be marked, desiring with our deepest desire, that the serenity of his famous name may not be clouded, nor that the prosperity of his state should be torn in any way, or be touched in a costly manner, bowed down by the prayers of the devout N. they possess, or in the future they will be able to obtain by means of justice, under our special protection, in imitation of the divine emperors who preceded us, and the kings of the Romans, the aforesaid privileges, as they have been noted above, and the whole and each of their articles, all in addition donations, indulgences, thanks, liberties, and The rights of the brothers of the aforesaid order were duly and providentially delivered and granted by Frederick, the last emperor of the Romans, our predecessor of illustrious memory. None, then, etc.

LETTER XXVII. *The Patriarch of Jerusalem urges Rudolph to take the passage, having been exposed to the dangers of the Holy Land. (An. Dom. 1285, cod. Rud. XXVII.)*

ARGUMENT.--The Patriarch of Jerusalem, and the officials of the Holy Land, being in dire need of help against the sultan of Babylon, who with an immense army was penetrating to the borders of his province, filling everything with terror, and preparing innumerable devices for the assault of the cities, turned to the power of Rudolph, supplicants, and exposed the imminent dangers, and fearing a future crisis, they ask for timely assistance before the general passage.

Most excellent, etc. Brother Thomas, etc., with the devout recommendation of the Holy Land, themselves, and salvation in him who for the salvation of the human race deigned to be mercifully crucified at Jerusalem. How much more gloriously the divine power exalted your majesty, and how much more abundantly in gifts of graces the omnipotence of the eternal Son of the King of the world raised you among the rest of the world, so much more confidently does he turn to the refuge of your serenity in those things that touch the business of the crucified, and so much more promptly the timely support of your summit, for the preservation of this and since, as the unquestionable credulity of all holds firmly, thinking successfully of directing the business of this land, and therefore longing to be informed more frequently of its state, a certain presence only, and briefly, which shakes the natives of this land with a kind of continuous fluctuation, retained in the past in silence, lest the length of the narrative should offend the royal hearing, we announce to your majesty the present handwritten note. Let your royal highness know, therefore, that the enemy of Egypt, with his immense army, has at last come out from the borders of Babylonia, and advancing as far as the neighboring places to us, and with his usual cunning now towards Armenia, now towards Tripoli, but also [sitting] now near Tire and Akon. and running through other places of ours, he devises grave plots for us and for the whole province, and rightly fearing a speedy experience of his forces on account of our fewness, he threatens the equipment necessary for the capture of the cities, and other things suitable to his infinite army, diligently preparing. But what future days may bring forth, upon whom he aims the bow of his perversity, or who may be the future outcome of things foreseen, we are anxious under the distresses of rushing dangers, and as if under the sword of an enemy [the sun] placed under the sword, let us continually fear the onslaught of fury. However, breathing in the help of your mighty right hand, for which all the people of Cismarinus pour out continuous prayers to the Lord, we unanimously implore your preeminence, inasmuch as assuming the task of the royal magnificence of the aforesaid land trodden by the feet of Christ and reddened with his most holy blood, do not deign for its custody in the meantime, until by the general let a passage be delivered from the jaws of the enemy of Christ, from a competent and opportune one to provide him with relief from so many fluctuating dangers. May your royal majesty live and prosper for a long time, to whom we most devoutly recommend the business of the aforesaid land.

LETTERS

LETTER XXVIII. *Rudolph writes to the bishop of Trent about an amicable settlement to be made with the Count of Tyrol. (An. Dom. 1276, cod. Rud. XXVIII.)*

ARGUMENT.--When Rudolph had received to settle the dispute between the bishop of Trent and Meinhard, count of Tyrol and Goria, over certain camps and revenues, and had issued Laud, to whom the bishop did not stand burdened by dictating himself, and in the meantime both had failed to obey, when it was most necessary, now at last she completely He is about to make up the inconveniences of his Church, and he proposes to him a very useful opportunity, promising that he will not depart from what is fair and just.

Rudolphus, etc., to the venerable bishop of Trent, etc. If, having attended to our labors, which we have done to the questions of you and the noble Count of Tyrol, he had answered more favorably to the fruits of amicable agreement, and if both of you had looked more serenely at the fact that we were not busying ourselves with our progress, but with your interests in the same negotiations, the Roman Empire in this time of its necessity and yours it would have been dear to us, nor would our sincere intention, which served your interests, have suffered the interpreters of the left voice. And although the judgment of our mind, having been carefully examined by discussions, tells us nothing else, than that in every part, as far as it was possible for us, we were careful and looked forward to your justice, yet you, as it is said, complain that you are burdened by us, and cause offense, not bearing our innocence. , who several times put you in place of our defense as a shield. Of course, if experience and difficult events have taught you that our plans have drawn you to your own advantage and advancement, still be at peace with our counsel, and bear with the departure, that your church may be restored to us, beset by grave dangers, by our intervening; you have not submitted at all. There is, indeed, by the grace of God, a full possibility and will, that we may cut off the matter of discord to both of you, provided that it pleases you to rest with the same purpose that we always propose to follow the truth, and that we shall not be more indifferent to your rest and advantage because your contention rests on some injury to us.

LETTER XXIX. *Rudolph writes to the Queen of France about renewing her homage. (An. Dom. 1274, cod. Rud. XXIX.)*

ARGUMENT.--When Berengarius, count of the province, had died without male issue, and had not been allowed to obtain the county of the province and Forkalquer during the interregnum by fiduciary right from the king of the Romans, as of the right of the empire, Margaritha Berengarius' eldest daughter, through her orator Rudolph, had paid tribute to Rudolph, promising to renew it to the same orator, whom Rudolph sends with a plenipotentiary to demand tribute and other conditions in the name of the kingdom.

Rudolph, etc. The illustrious Queen of France, etc. It may be that by the industrious man N., whom you long ago brought to our presence for your reception, and the name of procurator then vacant for us, and the Roman Empire assigned to the counties of N. and the principalities of N. Oath of homage and loyalty due. However, since the concession and reception of the same principalities were preceded by agreements of this kind, that the same oath of fidelity and homage, as soon as you should happen to be required of us in this name of ours, you would personally renew with our solemn message. Behold, we assign the honorable N. to the presence of your highness in the debt of faith, which binds you to us and to the government, requiring you to be present in succession, inasmuch as in our turn and in our name, you solemnly renew the oath of fidelity and homage owed to us on the premises. The conditions which the said N. also at that time interjected to us and the same Roman government in the same way in the person of the aforesaid N. are to be liberally fulfilled according to the fact that the same governor has led them to demand them. For we pour into him the plenitude of power over all the premises, and to those who look to the premises, to be satisfied by all promises and to accept whatever has been ordered, or even procured, by the oft-said presupposition in the premises of all and each, as if it happened to be presented in our own person.

LETTER XXX. *Rudolph writes to the archbishop that he may judge justly. (An. Dom. 1280, cod. Rud. 30).*

ARGUMENT.--Archbishop N., to whom, as the supreme prince of the empire, together with the other privileges, had confirmed the right of life and death throughout his dominion, he exhorts him to judge according to the example of the supreme eternal king, without any acceptance of persons, as he certainly has royal power and authority, if need be. I would not be lacking in just his opinions.

Rudolph, etc. No. archbishop, etc. By the grant of your Majesty, with whom our Serenity long ago invested you at No. place, you received full and free power to judge in your districts and territories, after the manner of our great princes in civil and criminal cases. For since we know that you are one of the noble princes of the Roman empire, we do not want anyone to doubt that mere government is annexed to your leadership, by which you have the right to attack criminal men and the power of the sword, but to be exercised by another, as befits your order and honor. Moreover, since, according to the legitimate sanctions, the crime takes away all immunity and takes away every privilege, we want and command that, in so far as those who are deprived of every privilege, nobility, or dignity, you judge with a just judgment, and you make the criminals to be judged according to the quality of the crimes, both in their capacities and in their persons [punishing]. You, therefore, putting on the form of a good governor, to whose concern it is chiefly concerned, that the province entrusted to him be purged of evil men, girt manfully to judge without selection and distinction of persons, looking upon the empire of the eternal king, who commanded, saying: Thus shall ye judge the great and the small, and do not doubt that because of let us bring the royal power, if need be, to carry out your just decisions which you have brought forward. For it is contrary to our purpose and to the Roman laws, that in punishing any criminal for a crime, the royal authority is specially required, since, according to the statutes, not the crimes of the Roman princes, but the revenge of the crimes, are to be brought to the royal ears.

LETTER XXXI. *Rudolph allows certain mountains to be cultivated. (An. Dom. 1280, cod. Rud. XXXI.)*

ARGUMENT.--Alberto Lincke and his associates, having a mine of silver, allows them to be cultivated, with the burden of paying the treasury of the region, according to the customary rights.

In the course of time, human memory recedes from what authority does not confirm, and the evidence does not confirm in literature. In consideration of this, our serenity, and what we have decided to do about certain silver mines, we thought worthy to be noted in the present letter. Let the people of the present age know, as well as the succession of future generations, that we have granted the said Albertus Lincke and his associates to cultivate the mountains, etc., and to serve them for their use. So that the rights of the same mountains, which also from other cultivators of similar mountains, are paid to us, etc. In whose, etc.

LETTER XXXII. *Rudolph recommends a certain abbot to the bishop. (An. Dom. 1274, cod. Rud. XXXII.)*

ARGUMENT.--When the abbey, the abbot of which was the prince of the empire, was vacant, and two men were striving to attain it, which suggested to Rudolph the desire of the dead prince and the crisis of that church, the same king of the Romans again and again commends him to the bishop of Constantia, who was in the possession of the church, as a man of providence and the consolation of the future for the good and the church.

In order that you, like us, could recognize with the open-eyed faith of my inquisitive mind, how many hardships and pressures the sacred Roman empire is shaken by, shaken by the pillars from which the same empire had to receive the strength to stand; these pressures in the abbey of N. on two persons laboring in opposition for the same, affect the senses of each one to such an extent that not only do we bear the failure of such a prince, but also the church itself, if it lacks a quick subsidization, should be perpetual charity in the hope of recovering salvation. We speak this out of compassion, and we say with the utmost awareness of the truth, that N., now existing in the possession of the church itself, knows and is able to preside over and benefit himself, and through his care the said church may reach its former state of happiness. You therefore, reverend father, most sincerely friends, having regard to the cause of justice of the aforesaid N. himself, as far as you can with God and honesty, endeavor to promote our kingdoms with a view, so that the aforesaid church is as provident and as proof as we believe it to be, and from certain by the signs we know, let the shepherd rejoice, and, cast off by sorrows, deserve to receive the benefits of consolation through him and us.

LETTERS

LETTER XXXIII. *Rudolph sympathizes with someone and comforts him. (An. Dom. 1277, cod. Rud. XXXIII.)*

ARGUMENT.--A prince, or a count, placed in straits by the rivals of the empire, excuses himself for not being able to help himself by raising an army, and consoles him with the hope of possible relief.

The honorable man N., our beloved acquaintance, ardent zealous for your honor, explained to us the immense pressures and various distresses of persecutions, with which, of course, in these days of stormy tempestuous weather, a storm has troubled you. Upon which indeed we could not help feeling the inconveniences of internal compassion, as we were waiting for your peace and tranquility with votive affection. From these, therefore, we draw a certain probable conjecture, that you cannot, as you desire, at this time enable yourself to lend yourself to our services and needs. Therefore, let your sincerity be known as constant, that we intend to aspire to your relief and to bear your disquiet, as best we can, in a good way.

LETTER XXXIV. *Rudolph grants the prince some ability to mint money. (An. Dom. 1280, cod. Rud. xxxiv.)*

ARGUMENT.--Diploma of the power given to bishop N., the prince of the empire, to mint money; by which it is commanded to be admitted throughout the whole empire, provided it be lawful.

Although we ought to extend the right hand of our beneficence to all the faithful of the Roman empire, yet the princes, as excellent bases on which the highness of the empire rests mightily, deserve a special prerogative to elevate us, and to extend the favors of our beneficence. It is for our sake that we want the whole world, both posterity and present, to accept us and accept the peaceful submission of grateful devotion, which has been spent on us up to now and will be able to be spent by N., more acceptable to us and to the holy government, looking more kindly, and for this reason greatly desiring, as he and that the episcopate of his votives may rejoice in the advantages and prosper in continuous increase, that the same N. in the city of N. freely coin legal coins, we freely and willingly nod to him from the royal liberality, and grant the present as we have thought, to each and every one established under the district of the Roman empire, giving this royal edict, they were more strict in their commands, that they should not fail to reverently admit the currency itself, as far as it existed legally, after all contradictions had been put aside.

LETTER XXXV. *Rudolph ordered that the coin, the coinage of which he had granted to a certain nobleman, the coinage, should be received without any hindrance. (An. Dom. 1280, cod. Rud. 35.)*

ARGUMENT.--He makes a certain noble ability to coin money, which he commands to be admitted, provided it is legal, in all the states and places existing in the same jurisdiction.

The potentate of august magnificence, thirsting for the increase of the honor of the empire, willingly enables and inclines himself to the advancement and advantages of those who, by their magnanimity, are visible towards the sacred empire of faith, glowing with a brighter light. Of course, since the noble N. obtained by his illustrious merits from the royal majesty that he may be permitted to strike perpetually within the district of his land a legal coinage coin by our permission and the royal plenitude of power, we commit and command to your university by the royal authority of the district, in so far as the coin itself formed by legal impression, which Whereupon the nobleman did the same, as has been expressed above, in your places and states reverently endeavor to admit, permitting alternate trades, and them to be carried on more freely, ceasing every hindrance.

LETTER XXXVI. *Rudolph confirms the privilege of a certain monastery. (An. Dom. 1281, cod. Rud. 36.)*

ARGUMENT.--Rudolph grants to the monastery of Zweytal the free passage of two tons of salt through the Danube: which privilege had long ago been granted to it by Frederick, duke of Austria.

The imperial throne is exalted, and the title of Augustus is adorned, when a kind consideration is extended to religious places, and their status and comforts are promoted by liberal munificence. For this reason we want it to be known to our faithful, both modern and all posterity, that those who are present at Vienna, promoting the successful growth of our summit by the Lord, and subjecting the leadership of Austria and Styria to our dominion by a prosperous lot, the abbot and convent of N. privilege from the said monastery clemently canceled our They presented it to His Highness, imploring us to renew the very privilege of transcribing it word for word, and to confirm what is contained in it by our grace. Whose tenor, etc. We, therefore, who are obliged to increase the state of the churches and increase the comforts of religious places by pious favor, have ordered the privilege itself to be inserted word for word in the present privilege, confirming the details contained in it of the imperial grace, we have established and sanctioned in a perial edict, that no person high or a lowly person, ecclesiastical or secular, presumes to trouble the aforesaid abbot and assembly of the monastery named above, contrary to the tenor of our present privilege, by a rash venture, etc.

LETTERS

LETTER XXXVII. *Rudolph restored the infamous to its former rank. (An. Dom. 1280, cod. Rud. 37.)*

ARGUMENT.--For a certain grave crime, the sentence of proscription does not merely remit the penalty of the crime, but it erases the crime itself. Wherefore he decreed that he should be free from every mark of infamy, and restored him whole, as if he had never been subject to any crime.

We continue the noble work of him who sits on the throne, urging clemency. If we fall through the slippery delirium of guilt, our hands are quickly enabled to relieve the remedies, and we indulge in the burdens of forgiveness after the guilt, so that while we know that the crimes derived from the first parent have flowed into the posterity in the natural norm of transgression, we gladly bestow the gracious votes of reparation on the victims. For our sake we want them all, that when N. had been condemned by the dictates of justice for the infamy of some injurious sentence of proscription, we considering from the prerogative of our innate humanity that if there were no guilt, there would be no place for pardon, and desiring to moderate the rigor of justice with the seasoning of mercy. especially since after the injury has been satisfied, we fully and completely restore the aforesaid N. of royal meekness to its former order, commanding the tenor of the present, that it be admitted as before to all civil and public acts.

LETTER XXXVIII. *When Rudolph died, he replaced another procurator in the Roman court. (An. Dom. 1280, cod. Rud. XXXVIII.)*

ARGUMENT.--He deplores the death of Master Paulus de Interamna, the orator, or his procurator at the holy see, and with the most dutiful words, deplores his cardinal friend, who has replaced him with mature advice, and entrusts him to promote his affairs.

Presented to us lately from the mournful death of a pious record. N., drawing with tearful sobs the cup of exceedingly bitter bitterness, while we consider inwardly that we have suffered an irreparable loss from his loss, we resort with diligent meditation to the only counsel, from which the hand of the Most High pierced us with such a grievous puncture, and deprived us of such a watchful promoter, trusting in you let us gather together the sum of all our actions, in order that we may sincerely consult the needs of our friends, both of whom we know and wish, and to assist them in a remedial manner. Therefore, placing in you the anchor of our hope after God above all, we beseech your most pious fatherhood, inasmuch as you are willing to be present with salutary counsels and timely aids in promoting and facilitating our affairs.

LETTER XXXIX. *The king of Cyprus writes to Rudolph that he writes to him about his successes. (An. Dom. 1275 cod. Rud. xxxix.)*

ARGUMENT.--The King of Cyprus, desiring greatly to know Rudolph's happiness, the future consolation of the unhappy state of the Holy Land, desires to be told by him how the business of relief for the Holy Land will proceed. Then, as he writes, announcing that he is a guest, he wishes to hear the same about him. He says that he will hear some innovations made in Syria, as well as some other secrets from the ambassador he sends.

Most excellent, etc. King of Cyprus, etc. Since we are affected with continual desires to hear the wishes of the success of your magnificent state, the success of which would undoubtedly give way to great consolation for the tearful events of the Holy Land, we implore your imperial excellency, with the affection we can, in so far as the successful events of the things that are happening around us, which we wish to progress with unceasing increases, to us more often By your noble letters you would like to express your good pleasure and commands in confidence. Knowing that in the making of the present we were fully flourishing through the grace of God, with the longing of our hearts, we desire to hear the same affectionately about your magnificence, and, if it were possible, to look at you with more affectionate eyes. But the state of the aforesaid Holy Land, and those things which are now renewed, will be able to know and understand through your Majesty's imperial magnificence, and certain things which we have enjoined upon him to be proposed.

LETTER 40. *Rudolph the Patriarch of Jerusalem for the relief of the Holy Land. (An. Dom. 1275, cod. Rud. XL.)*

ARGUMENT.--The Patriarch of Jerusalem and the offices of the Holy Land again ask for help from Rudolph, whom, as he is not ignorant of the affairs of Syria, they implore more earnestly to have mercy on the necessity and want of the nobles and the people. The Babylonian tyrants tell of their cruelty against the Christians of Armenia, and they say that the camp gathered in the region of Antiochene spread terror widely, so that, leaving the weakest places, they all fled to the fortified places, which were fitted for strength to repel the fury of the enemy. He was unable to relieve other people's distress except with tears; that they lacked many kinds of munitions to resist a most powerful enemy, and that they would perish unless timely help came. They send an ambassador, a knight who had been a long time in Syria and commend him again and again to Rudolph.

LETTERS

To the most excellent and powerful prince, etc. Brother Thomas, a humble stranger in Jerusalem, Ballianus, the chief steward of the kingdom of the Jerosolvites. and viceroy of the kingdoms of Jerusalem and Cyprus, etc. with the recommendation of the Holy Land they executed themselves. We do not believe that the royal majesty is aside, as much as it is necessary for the remainder of the Christian community to be guarded by precautions against hostile intrigues, by fortifications against the indescribable power of the tyrant, by remedies and protections against the dragon virus, by which the whole region is confused. We also do not believe that the Patriarch of Jerusalem, a humble and religious house, and others as noble as the plebeians, whose condition and rank, because of the past crises of wars, the malice of times, the devastation of places, and the various cases of poverty of the people, are oppressed by the great amount of poverty, and how much they are affected by miseries and extreme want. article, no respite was given to them, and they were crushed by no supporting support in the circumstances of such great dangers. Finally, we do not want you to be on the other side, to what extent the Egyptian enemy, due to the insufficiency of the forces on our part, was raised to the pride, which cruelly wet the same with his hands, and with the sword in the blood of Christ's faithful, miserably in the kingdom of Armenia for a period of twenty days, about the destruction of the living, the burning of towns and cities, and the final depopulation of all that could impetuously reach him, he debauched; there he unmercifully fulfilled the fury of his long-conceived fury, and with his kingdom disintegrated and utterly desolate, he arrived in the country of Antiochene, and there, as is reported, he remained with his whole powerful army, but it was entirely unknown to all to what his intention was directed, or to what his unbridled will intoxicated by the triumphs of the past and moistened by the spoils of the faithful, he is driven more often. Therefore, from these and other infinite dangers and fears, through various letters and special messages faithfully intimated to the king, by whom we are shaken to the very heart and foundations, our places, which we trust to be able to withstand the fury of the enemy by our situation and the help of our warriors, are fortified, according to the capabilities of the defenders. , and their inhabitants, not without great loss of property and bodily distress, flee to safer places with their children, belongings, and relatives, and abandon their own homes. Moreover, with their miseries and sufferings, from whom and upon whom we are required in various ways, and frequently, importunately and importunately, we are unable to come to the aid of the necessary remedies, we are pierced by the bitterness of pain, and into a lack of strength, compassion, or affection, we shed tears of charity. Indeed, your excellency knows the strength of the inhabitants of Syria, and the deplorable state of the province of Cismarinus, he knows, moreover, the power of the Egyptians, he also knows the extreme poverty of the aforesaid patriarch of Jerusalem, and the poverty of all the religious, he knows, in addition to this, how many fortifications of walls, machines, garrids, helmets, and the abundance of warlike instruments of the holy land our defenses need to be fortified, he knows that we lack a sufficient number of defenders, and that we have neither from ourselves nor from any other powerful forces for supplies, so that we can provide both ourselves and the weak places with the aforesaid defenses from the opportune and competent support. Let us, therefore, beseech the clemency of such a great king concerning the exposed dangers of the children, may the right hand of your power come to the aid of a speedy remedy for us surrounded by the snares of ravenous wolves, the blessed royal hand palpate our wounds and wounds, infusing them with salutary ointments of mercy, before their sanity clings to their marrow. We recommend Mr. Elias de Insat, a soldier who is present, and who has been in the land for a long time, more inclined to your greatness. May his royal majesty live and prosper for a long time, to whom we most devoutly commend ourselves and the Holy Land.

LETTER XLI. Rudolph takes a five-year-old boy under his protection. (An. Dom. 1280, cod. Rud. 41.)

ARGUMENT.--Rudolphus the orphan, who has not yet passed the fifth year of his age, is taken under royal protection; and all his property, both movable and immovable, declares by this diploma that he has undertaken to protect the region under the patronage of the whole empire.

For this purpose, the leadership has been placed on our shoulders of royal dignity, and our weapons have been anointed with the oil of sacred libation, so that with a hand of strength and an outstretched arm we may be the defenders of all who live under the Roman empire. But even though we are bound to all this by the care of the government we have undertaken, yet we especially want and must protect those whom the divine oracle has more especially committed to our protection, crying out with the precept: Thou shalt be a helper to the ward and the orphan. Indeed, our beloved N., deprived of parental comfort, not only because of his pupil status, but also because of the tenderness of his childhood, since he is not yet five years old, cannot defend or help himself. For the same reason we receive them under our protection, asserting all their movable and immovable goods under the shield of our defense, protection, and protection. Wherefore we command all the faithful of the Roman Empire under the cover of our grace, that no one dare invade the said child, or his property, or disturb in any way. But if anyone presumes to do this, let him know that he will be punished in such a way that his punishment will be a terror to the rest.

LETTERS

LETTER 42. *Rudolph asks with something. (An. Dom. 1277, cod. Rud. XLII.)*

ARGUMENT.--Rudolphus, having received the letter of N. rebellis, who removed from himself the guilt of treachery, with the vain obstinacy of suspicion and reproaches brought upon him, wrote back that he would bear with patience the same affections he had received from other graver injuries;

If your letter had proceeded from the well of an intact breast, upon the abominable business of perfidy, it would not have charged innocent hands, nor killed a faithful heart with the sting of a stinging suspicion. But because it often happens, which I do not think has any place among you, that what one feels about himself is suspected of another, I protect myself against such hostile injection attacks with the shield of patience, girded and fortified with the armor of temperance. In truth I did not believe that I should suffer these things from my rival, nor should I suffer such outrageous insults from the enemy, especially since, if you remember, I had endured much more serious injuries from you before these times. But in order that the integrity of my irreproachable innocence should come out to the public, I believed you were satisfied by N. Which, of course, with the desired effect being lacking, I asked you to do otherwise.

LETTER 43. *Rudolph writes against the unduly exacting tax. (An. Dom. 1280, cod. Rud. 43.)*

ARGUMENT.--The publicans and tax collectors who demand taxes from the newcomers unduly, and collect them unjustly, order them to desist from illegal activities, lest the peace established everywhere be disturbed.

The earth rose up against you with cries, and the groans of the poor entered the ears of the royal highness, and because of the fact that they resisted the general observation of the peace by the heel of the rebellion, instead of your free will, they presumed to extort the toll from the passers-by, and without ceasing to burden them with taxes. We affectionately require and urge your prudence, commanding you nevertheless by royal authority, in so far as you restrain your hands from unlawful work, and reflect upon what is lawful. Otherwise, we want you to know as a matter of fact that we will sharpen all our energies, cares and minds to the beauty of this kind of peace, so that it may flourish again with its former beauty.

LETTER XLIV. *Rudolph recommends someone for a certain ecclesiastical benefit. (An. Dom. 1280, cod. Rud. XLIV.)*

ARGUMENT.--For the provision of N. to his reporter, nay, on the other hand, he thanks the bishop of Leodiens; and he declares that it will be the most pleasing thing to him, by which the contributor will earn royal patronage for himself and his church, if he makes spontaneous promises. And he nodded, that having obtained the provision, either by residing in the church, he should serve the same laudably, or, by order of the contributor, by remaining in the royal court, look after the business of that and the church.

We were greatly pleased at the display of your devotion, for the fact that we and the Roman Empire respected the steadfastness of the pure faith, by providing for our beloved correspondent N., nay, rather, you gave us such a laudable hope of his provision in your church. We expect you to be more and more fully aroused in the culture of our dominion by this, and we long for the more votive for his progress, in whose fruitful submissions we have been well pleased. And surely you will render so acceptable and so peaceful a service to our serenity by the promotion of the same, which we conceive to be incessantly present to you and to the same church in all opportunities, and to aspire to favorable desires. Therefore, in order that your laudable preconceived intention regarding your promises may be fulfilled with a spirit of more prompt study and be pursued with a more skillful benevolence, we willingly nod to your sincerity, that when the said N. has obtained the favor of divine favor clemency, in the planter of the foreordained church, like a fruitful seedling of residence, it will bear the desired fruit, unless perhaps it may also happen that the same will be more usefully engaged in managing your business and that of your church in our court by commanding you.

LETTER LXV. *Rudolph writes about a certain rebellion. (An. Dom. 776, cod. Rud. 45.)*

ARGUMENT.--Meinhard, as it seems, writes to the count of Tyrol about the old discord, which he was intervening with the bishop of Tridentine, to whom he says that he was deputed as an interpreter of the peace to be reconciled; but afterwards he changed his plan, when he found that the discord had grown stronger. He prays the same to state the state of the question, and to lay down his counsel, that a suitable remedy may be brought.

At N.'s departure from our presence we believed that he had arranged such an arrangement between you and himself, that he could scarcely have ever ascended into our hearts, that he would in some way raise the heel of rebellion against you. But when we heard this, as if we were greatly surprised, nay, astonished, the matter turned to the contrary; would inseparably connect you and N. himself. It is true that a certain hostile rumor sounded in our ears, by which the release of the said N. was retarded. Wherefore we send you the exhibitor of the present, requesting with the greatest affection that we can, that you will at once inform us of the state and conditions of the business, and give your plan, how we may be able to put to rest the folly of the resentment which has arisen by a suitable remedy.

LETTER XLVI. *Rudolph recommends a certain literate. (An. Dom. 1283, cod. Rud. 46.)*

ARGUMENT.--Desiring to honor his courtier, distinguished by letters and morals, for his merits, and therefore concerned about his promotion to the episcopal seat; because, being hindered by many affairs, he cannot by himself, he calls N. as part of his concern, and entrusts the whole matter to him.

The usual benevolence of royal munificence distinguishes the merits of persons by the dispensation thus provided, so that those who shine with a more splendid luster in the knowledge of letters, manners, and conversation, he brings out the grace of favor with greater grace, and endeavors to honor with more abundant favors. It is true that the prudent and honorable man N., walking amiably in the royal house with consent, has practiced so exceptionally with his diffused treasure of skill around us and ours, and still continues to practice the works of honesty, that we are bound to exalt him with the beneficences of special grace, and to exalt him with appropriate honors; because, nevertheless, the frequent and busy gathering of the influence of our actions, which usually leaps about our sides, does not allow us to think about its promotion, according to the desires of our mind, while the time enables itself to this purpose, obtaining confidence from your prudence, that through you it is worth redeeming the negligence already We leave it to your discretion to commit defaults, etc.

LETTERS

LETTER LXVII. *Rudolph approves certain chapters against heresies issued by the emperor Frederick. (Ann. Dom. 1280, cod. Rud. 47.)*

ARGUMENT.--The royal authority confirms the constitution against heresies issued by Frederick II on the day of his coronation, with the encouragement and approval of Honorius III, the supreme pontiff; and he binds himself and all those constituted in the Roman Empire to its observance.

Rudolph, by the grace of God, was always Augustus, king of the Romans. To all the faithful of Christ, please check the present page for the health of the undersigned. Since the pestilential cunning of heretical cunning, abominable to God and hateful to men, which stain the sheep of Dominic's flock with their contagion, we unceasingly persecute the detestable scumbags like the furs of bitterness, and for this reason I would like to extend to their extirpation all the power of the sword entrusted to us by God. The emperor, our predecessor, issued against heretics, which we saw intact, not canceled, not abrogated, and not in any part defective, consigned with his seal, we took it to be noted by those present, decreeing that they should be faithfully observed by all who are considered to be of Christian profession. And the tenor of such constitutions is as follows: They begin, etc. We, therefore, who for the protection of the Catholic faith principally, as witness of the Most High, have assumed the honor and the burden of the royal dignity, set forth all and every one for the eradication of this kind of nefarious sect, and the strengthening of the Christian faith piously and providentially instituted we solemnly approve, and bind ourselves to the same observances by the testimony of those present, desiring and commanding that these same things be firmly and inviolably observed by all to whom the Roman dominion extends. In whose testimony, etc.

LETTERS

The Scriptorium Project is the work of a small group of lay people of various apostolic churches who are interested in the preservation, transmission, and translation of the works of the early and medieval church. Our efforts are to make the works of the church fathers accessible to anyone who might have an interest in Christian antiquities and the theological, philosophical, and moral writings that have become the bedrock of Western Civilization.

To-date, our releases have pulled from the Greek, Syriac, Georgian, Latin, Celtic, Ethiopian, and Coptic traditions of Christianity, and have been pulled from sundry local traditions and languages.

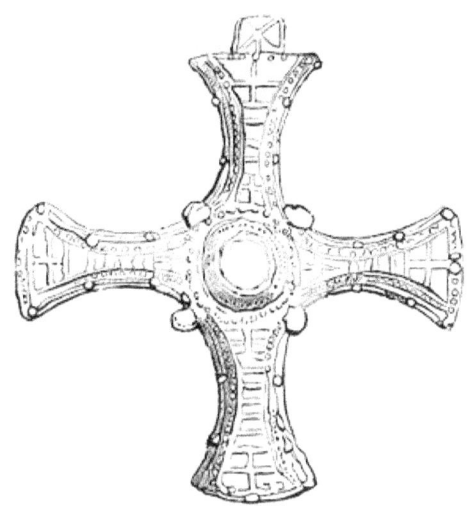

Other Selections from the Medieval German Church Series:

Letters by Rudolf I Habsburg, Holy Roman Emperor (Dec. 2012)

About Fifteen Problems (De quindecim problematibus) by St. Albertus Magnus (Feb 2022)

On Fate (De Fato) by St. Albertus Magnus (Feb 2023)

www.ingramcontent.com/pod-product-compliance
Lightning Source LLC
LaVergne TN
LVHW021828060526
838201LV00058B/3557